THE REAL WITCHES' COVEN

THE REAL WITCHES' COVEN

The Definitive Guide to Forming

Your Own Wiccan Group

KATE WEST

LLEWELLYN

Published in 2009 by Llewellyn Publications

First published by Thorson's, an imprint of HarperCollinsPublishers in 2003

Illustrations by Chris Down

Llewellyn is a registered trademark of Llewellyn Worldwide, Ltd.
Library of Congress Cataloging-in-Publication Data available upon request

Published by Thorsons 2003

ISBN-13:978-0-7387-1582-7

Llewellyn Worldwide does not participate in, endorse, or have any authority or
responsibility concerning private business transactions between our authors and the public.
All mail addressed to the author is forwarded but the publisher cannot, unless specifically
instructed by the author, give out an address or phone number. Any Internet references
contained in this work are current at publication time, but the publisher cannot guarantee
that a specific location will continue to be maintained. Please refer to the publisher's website
for links to authors' websites and other sources.

Llewellyn Publications
A Division of Llewellyn Worldwide, Ltd.
2143 Wooddale Drive, Dept. 978-0-7387-1927-6
Woodbury, Minnesota 55125-2989, U.S.A.
www.llewellyn.com

Printed in China.

CONTENTS

DEDICATION

This book is dedicated to all those who have taken on the task of running a Coven, and most especially to those who run the many Daughter Covens of the Hearth of Hecate. It is through your energy, dedication and hard work that the Craft continues.

ACKNOWLEDGEMENTS

There is a huge amount of available material on the Craft, some of which is in print, but a lot of which is still passed down by word of mouth. As a result it is not always possible to attribute sources correctly. Nowhere is this more difficult than in the case of the poetry and chants which so many of us use, adapt or draw inspiration from. However, I would like to take the opportunity here to thank all those who have contributed, and those who are still contributing, to the collective wisdom of the Craft. I am especially grateful to those who did so in the days before it was as easy or acceptable to publish such works.

I would also like to thank all those who have more personally enabled me to produce this book, so:

Loving thanks go to my patient, loving husband and partner Steve, and our growing son Taliesin, who is beginning to understand that mummy is not having more fun on the computer than she would do at the park!

Grateful thanks to: Debbie, Keith and Lizzie for the proofreading, and to Chris for the illustrations. To Mike and Dave for keeping me supplied with working computers when the gremlins struck! To Natalie and Rocky for giving me some child-free time.

Last but not least, thank you to everyone at Element who has encouraged and supported me.

INTRODUCTION

Merry Meet, and welcome to the Real Witches' Coven. Many people who have discovered the Craft seek to join with others in the celebration of the seasons and the working of magic. To do this they have either to find a suitable group or to establish a group of their own. In this book I intend to look at the complexities of running a Coven, both from the perspective of starting from 'scratch' and the ongoing organization and development of a group. Whilst the bulk of the book is addressed to the High Priestess and/or High Priest who runs the Coven, I am aware that many of you will be reading this with the intent of gaining an understanding into how a Coven works, with a view to being a successful Coven member. For those of you in this latter category Chapter Ten, 'The Good Covenor' gives an outline of some of the things that those running a Coven are looking for. There are also some contact addresses at the end of the book to help you locate a Coven in the first place.

So, you want to start a Coven? I did a 'straw poll' of a number of High Priestesses and High Priests and they all made the same comment: 'Don't do it!' This is because running a Coven is a lot of hard work and can be a lot of worry. On the other hand it is also hugely rewarding, you get to watch the progress of newcomers, see their personal and spiritual development and ultimately see some of them go on to form their own Covens. It is a joy when the group comes together to perform Rituals with depth and meaning, and to work magic which is powerful and effective. There is little which compares with the glow of pride and satisfaction you get when the Coven is all pulling together, when it grows and you can see the Craft continuing on in a meaningful way.

My intention here is to help you to avoid some of the pitfalls, and to give you a framework to help you organize your Coven I also hope to give you ways of dealing with the more common problems, and problem people, as well some ideas about solving those problems which do arise. Whilst this book may appear to dwell on the difficulties you might encounter, this is because I am attempting to help you deal with them; I'm assuming you will be able to enjoy your successes without any guidance!

I do not intend that you should slavishly follow the ideas given here, but rather that you can use them to develop your own style. There are almost as many ways of running a Coven as there are Covens, and only you can decide which methods you feel comfortable with. Furthermore, you may find that not only does your style change with time, but that it will have to adjust as different people join your group.

Some of you reading this book may feel that I seem to be somewhat dubious about what is, after all, a group of adults coming together to share a common aim. Some may feel that I advocate the High Priestess and/or High Priest taking control of every aspect of Covenors' lives, or even that I am on some kind of personal power trip. None of these represent my feeling, or my intent. Personally, I feel that we should all be grown-up enough to act responsibly and moreover, that over-regulation leads to stagnation. However, what I have written in this book not only represents my own experience as a High Priestess, but also that of the many other High Priestesses and High Priests with whom I have discussed the content. The examples I have given are all real events, featuring real people, which perhaps says something about the Covens and Covenors which I, and others, have come across!

Several people have asked me why my books are called 'The Real Witches' ...' I'd like to point out that this is not because I feel that my Craft is the only 'real' one. There cannot be a right or wrong way to practise the Craft, if it is to continue being a living belief system. As I have written elsewhere, so long as you hold the beliefs of the Witch you can call yourself Witch. Whether you choose to differentiate between Wicca and Witchcraft will be up to you, but I believe that, as the Craft develops and spreads we will find many different branches of Craft, all having the same roots. This is a strength of the Craft, for to remain static is to move backwards. In my books I endeavour to write about Witchcraft for people who live in the real world. That is, people who have jobs, partners, children, parents, homes to run, studies to complete, etc., and who cannot devote their every waking moment, or drop everything at a moment's notice, to study and practise the Craft. I feel very strongly that, for a Witch to be effective they should function as a part of life, not apart from it.

To avoid the somewhat clumsy terminology 'High Priestess and/or High Priest', 'she/he', 'her/his' etc., throughout this book I refer to the High Priestess as the person who runs the Coven. I apologize if this offends any High Priests but I feel that it will make for easier and more pleasant reading. In the Craft the role is in fact often shared by the High Priestess and the High Priest, and occasionally a Coven will be run by a High Priest alone, but you will find more on the roles within a Coven in Chapter One, The Family of the Witches.

Those of you with no previous knowledge or experience of Witchcraft will find a very brief explanation in Chapter One, and a list of Recommended Reading at the end of the book. But, whether you are running a Coven or would like to be; whether you are a member of a Coven or are looking to join one; even if you are just curious as to what they are and do, I hope that this book will prove not only useful but enjoyable too.

Blessed Be
Kate

 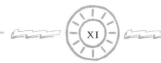

THE FAMILY OF THE WITCHES

What is a Coven? The term Coven is used to describe a group of Witches who meet and work together on a regular basis. Despite the common misconception, a Coven does not have to be 13 people, but is essentially any number from 3 upwards. A Witch on his or her own is termed a Solitary Witch. Two Witches working together are usually termed a Partnership, even when of the same gender. As with any group the Coven has to have a leader and this is usually the High Priestess, either supported by the High Priest or on her own. In some cases a Coven will be run by the High Priest, but this is usually because there is no Priestess of sufficient rank and experience to take the role of High Priestess.

Just as there are many different kinds of Witch there are different kinds of Coven. There are Gardnerian, Alexandrian, Hereditary and Traditional Covens, and even some which combine these and other aspects of the Craft. There are even cyber-Covens, although unless very well directed, these tend to be more of a forum where Solitaries can share ideas, seek magical assistance and generally discuss the Craft. There are some Covens which are single sex, although the majority

are mixed. Some are dedicated to specific pantheons of Gods, others are more eclectic. Some will take newcomers (often called Aspirants or Neophytes), some won't. Generally speaking, most Covens will initially follow the path that was learned by their High Priestess, although their practice will almost always evolve and differ from this in time. This is one of the reasons for the diversity of practice which can be found in the Craft.

There is no 'right' type of Coven, but it is important to find, or create, the kind that is right for you.

But what does a Coven do? Witches who have joined a Coven hold the same beliefs, celebrate the same festivals and work very similar magics to Witches who work alone. The difference is that they do these things together, whereas Solitaries rarely have the opportunity to meet together. This is not to say that those in a Coven don't work on their own, but solitary work by Coven members is supported by their High Priestess, and possibly the rest of the Coven. For those of you reading this who are uncertain of what today's Witches do, the following is a brief outline, similar to that found in *The Real Witches' Kitchen*. However, I would recommend also reading *The Real Witches' Handbook* for a more in-depth explanation of the Craft as well as an exploration of ways of working outside of the Coven system.

THE CRAFT

Witchcraft is one of a number of belief systems whose roots pre-date Christianity and which come under the heading of Pagan. Indeed, Witchcraft has roots which go back to the Neolithic period: countless items of evidence exist to demonstrate that Goddess-oriented belief has been prevalent throughout history. Having said that, the Craft is a living religion and has as much relevance to us today as it had

to its practitioners in the past. We still seek healing of our bodies and minds, strength to deal with our daily lives, understanding and compassion to help us relate to those around us, and to develop ourselves.

So what do Witches believe in and how do they express these beliefs? Witchcraft does not have the structure or form of many of the current orthodox religions. The Craft, in common with many Pagan beliefs, encourages free thought and intelligent debate of its belief systems and its place in our modern-day lives. Witchcraft has no formal priesthood, beyond those individuals that are respected or considered knowledgeable by others. In the Craft we are each our own Priest or Priestess and therefore make our own decisions as to the expression of our beliefs. As a result there is no 'one true way' to being a Witch. This gives rise to a great diversity in our daily practices, and indeed enables the Craft to grow and adapt to the real world in a way that other paths find difficult because of their interpreted doctrine. Having said that, there are many beliefs and practices that most Witches hold in common:

The belief that the Divine is both male and female, equal and in balance, and that we should seek that balance in ourselves and in our lives. Put simply this means that we believe in a Goddess and a God, and they may be referred to by many names, according to the needs of the individual or indeed their personal preference. It helps to think of the Divine as being like a faceted crystal, with each facet having a different identity, although all being part of the same principle of Divinity. As a result you may find that the Goddess is referred to as Hecate, Aradia, Ceridwyn, etc and that the God is referred to as Herne, Cernunos, Pan, etc. Some Witches will simply refer to the Lord and Lady or the Goddess and the God, and these are the terms that I will use in this book. Others will call them the Old Ones or the Old Gods, or even just the Gods.

The Goddess is seen as having three aspects: Maiden, Mother and Crone (or Wise One). These aspects are reflected in the cycle of the Moon, and in our daily lives, for everything has its beginning, middle and closing phases.

The God also has different aspects, and these are clearly defined through the festivals of the Wheel of the Year.

As mentioned above we have no formal Priesthood in the Craft although those Witches working in a group or Coven setting will have a High Priestess and High Priest who are the leaders of that group. This does not make them better Witches, it simply denotes their knowledge and ability within that group. The roles and responsibilities of the High Priestess and High Priest will be discussed in detail later in this book. We do not rely on others to interpret or intercede with our Gods for us, we are each entitled to make our own connection with the Divine, in our own way. This might be through ritual, meditation or magic and most Witches will use a combination of different techniques at different times.

Witchcraft does not rely on a key divine text, in the way that Christians have the Bible or Muslims the Koran. Much has been written on and about the Craft; it is up to those who wish to read these to make their own personal decisions as to their relevance. Each individual can choose the complexity of their Rituals, and the form that their path will take. For some this may mean working in a group or Coven, others may prefer a Solitary path. Some will seek to work formalized magic whilst others prefer the Hedgewitch approach, working closely with nature and using herbs to achieve their magics.

Everyone is entitled to their own informed choice of spiritual path, so long as they harm no-one else. Witchcraft does not preach or seek converts, we do not feel the need for everyone to believe as we do in order to feel secure in our faith. There is plenty of room in this world for everyone to find their own way of relating to the Divine. In fact all religions have much in common, many beliefs and religious stories have their mirror images across all faiths. Hence, there is no reason why we should not encourage and celebrate a diversity of beliefs. We encourage our young to examine many paths and to make their own decisions, based on their own needs. We do not seek to convert others to our beliefs, nor do we wish to be indoctrinated in turn.

We believe that we should tread lightly upon the Earth, not taking more than we need and indeed trying to recompense for that which we have taken. This involves trying to live our lives in the modern world and at the same time in balance with the planet. This does not mean that we are all 'green warriors' campaigning against the building of roads or houses. We try to live carefully and caringly.

THE ELEMENTS

Witches see themselves reflected by the elements of Air, Fire, Water, Earth and Spirit. Whilst these elements are all around us in nature they are also within us; air represents the intellect, fire is passion and enthusiasm, water equals emotion and feeling, earth is the body, and spirit is the self that binds all together. These are the energies we can harness in working magic and in order for this to work effectively we must be able to achieve balance between them. These elements also have reflections in daily life. For every project to work it must have its phases of thought, enthusiasm, emotional involvement and formation, and each step must also be imbued with its own spirit.

MAGIC

We believe in and practise Magic. Magic has been defined as the ability to create change by force of will and is very similar to the belief in the power of prayer held

by many of the orthodox faiths. However, we believe that with magic it is our personal intervention that creates the change around us, not the whim of some superior being. Magic is not like cookery, just a matter of following a recipe and getting a result. Magic requires a deep understanding of the self and the energies that are all around us, and the ability to control and focus our own energies.

One of the greatest keys to this is the ability to visualize. It also requires a study and understanding of the elements, not just in the world, but also within ourselves. The magic we practise is not that of stage conjuring or of the special effects that you see so often in modern films. It is practised to heal, protect and enhance our lives. It is worked for ourselves, our near and dear, and for those who come to us with requests for help. Magic should always be practised with regard to the law of threefold return which states that whatever you do, good or ill, will be returned to you three times over. The Law of Threefold Return is not confined to magical working, but applies to everything we do in our lives. It is also sometimes said that magic responds to need and not to desire. There are other concerns which should be taken into account before starting any magical working and these are detailed in *The Real Witches' Handbook*. However, if you are careful to harm no-one and not to interfere with anyone's freedom of will, then you have the basic guidelines for good magical practice.

THE WHEEL OF THE YEAR

Witches celebrate the Wheel of the Year. The Witches' calendar contains eight key festivals, called Sabbats. At these we mark the changes of the seasons and the sto-ries of the Goddess and the God. Whenever possible Witches will gather together to celebrate these festivals, to dance, sing and honour the Goddess and the God

by re-enactment of their stories. Often Covens will join together to celebrate the Sabbats, incorporating 'daughter' Covens and even Solitary Witches who are accepted by the group. Some Covens also use the lesser Sabbats as introductory rituals to which are invited potential new entrants, often called Aspirants. At the end of these rituals we celebrate by feasting with food and wines. Many of the Sabbats have a familiar feel to non-Witches as they have been taken over by newer belief systems and incorporated into their calendars.

PERSONAL DEVELOPMENT

We take personal responsibility for our lives. The main 'rule' in the Craft is called the Wiccan Rede: 'An it harm none, do what thou will.' This in itself includes not only our respect for others and the world around us, but also respect for our-selves. We believe that we cannot blame others for our thoughts, words and deeds, and that if we do wrong it is up to us to do our best to rectify it.

We seek personal development. There is much to learn in the world and in the Craft, we seek to expand our knowledge and extend our skills by personal effort. Within a Coven the High Priest and Priestess act as signposts and guides, but it is the journey of the self, not just learning by rote. All Witches are aware that they will never know enough, let alone all. This personal development also includes expanding our personal skills and attributes, 'ironing out' our personal misconceptions and problems, and working to become the best self we can. Witchcraft has been called 'a thinking person's belief system', as it involves a course of personal exploration and general study which never ceases. Within a Coven this study and learning can be facilitated and aided by the High Priestess and High Priest, but they cannot do it for you.

THE SUMMERLANDS AND REINCARNATION

Witches believe that we live many lives and between them we return to the Summerlands, a resting place where we review the lessons we have learned in the life we have just completed, and select the lessons to be learned in the life to come. When we speak of reincarnation we do not mean that we come back as the same person but rather that our spirit is born again. Whilst it can be interesting to research previous incarnations, and the information we acquire may illuminate aspects of our current lives, it is necessary to remember that the personal responsibility we also believe in means that we cannot blame our past(s) for our current problems. We must live in the present and work towards achievement in this life.

HERBLORE

Witches utilize the properties of plants and nature for healing and self-improvement, and in the course of our magic. Herbs, plants and spices can be used in food and drink, lotions and ointments, sachets and talismans, incenses and candles. They can be used in their natural state (as I write this I have Rosemary on my desk to aid my thoughts and concentration), dried or in oil form, as in Aromatherapy which has become so popular in recent years. If you would like to find out more about herblore then I recommend reading *The Real Witches' Kitchen* which has many recipes, ideas and suggestions for the use of natural healing and magic.

SACRED SPACE

Witches do not have special buildings in which they worship, in fact most Witches do not even have a room or a space set aside for working. Witches create their own working space wherever and whenever they need it, and this can be inside or out. This space is called the Circle, and it is created in several steps. These are, briefly speaking:

The invocation of the elements, which are the energies on which we draw.

The invitation of the Goddess and the God; the Divine, whose assistance we need to perform our working, and in whose honour we gather.

The drawing of a Circle large enough to contain those taking part and the actions they are there to perform. This is usually done on the psychic level rather than on the physical, although some will place markers to visibly show the boundary. The Circle is drawn clockwise (or Deosil) from the north-east point of the area, between Earth and Air, and overlaps at that point in order to ensure that it is complete. The Circle is there to contain the energy raised, until it is ready to be released, and to protect those within its boundaries from outside energies and distractions.

THE COVEN

A Coven will usually meet together for each of the eight Sabbats, and these will generally be celebratory meetings. Here we may re-enact the stories of the Goddess and the God, or take an aspect of that point in the Wheel of the Year and utilize it to aid us in our daily lives. A Coven will also meet for the 12 or 13 Full Moons, or Esbats, of the year. These are more often working meetings – this is the time that we work magic for ourselves, for those we know, for those who come to us for assistance, or for the land or people in general. However, magic can and will be worked at other times of the Lunar cycle, and indeed sometimes at the Sabbats. Some Covens will also meet at other points of the calendar, perhaps for magical workings, or perhaps for discussion and development. In our Coven we hold 'training' meetings at the New Moon. These are the times when we explore different aspects of the Craft, or things allied to it such as divination, herblore or even take a look at other spiritual paths.

But a Coven should really be more than just a group who meet regularly and work together: they should respect one another, both for their work within the Craft and as individuals. They should be able to accept one another, good and bad traits included. They should like one another well enough to resolve, or at least set aside, personal differences. They should support the group and its members, not just at meetings, but in daily life. And they should be not just prepared but willing to work together and share chores and burdens. In other words, the Coven is the family group of the Witches, in the way that a family should be, working and playing together, helping and supporting one another.

STARTING A COVEN

There are some good reasons for starting a Coven of your own: you may have been asked by your High Priestess to 'hive off' and form a subgroup of the main Coven, who are often referred to as daughter and mother Covens respectively. In this case I trust that you will already have experienced the joy and wonder of seeing others develop and grow in the Craft. You may have been unable to find one which suits you or which is within reasonable distance. You may have worked Solitary for a number of years and wish to share your love of the Craft with others, and cannot locate a suitable group. Whichever category you are in you may find, like many before you, that you feel actually drawn to share and hand on your Craft. Witches who form Covens for these reasons face a difficult but rewarding path, and generally speaking the Goddess and God will watch over and support them.

There are also a number of poor reasons: you enjoy telling people what to do and seek to be the 'top dog' or boss. You wish to exert power and control over others. You like the idea of the drama and theatrics of centre stage. You seek to make money from the Craft. You are certain your brand of Witchcraft is the right one, and should be imposed on everyone else. Covens formed for these reasons generally do not flourish, or at least not for long. They inevitably attract the disapproval of the Witchcraft community and invite the Law of Threefold Return upon their founders! Some even bring the Craft into disrepute.

So, before you take any further steps on this path you need to be entirely sure of your motivations. Are you doing this for the right reasons? Give this some thought, meditate on your reasons, ask the Goddess for guidance. Where possible ask other Witches for their thoughts. Now on to some of the more practical stuff:

THE ROLE OF THE HIGH PRIESTESS

A Coven is run by the High Priestess. Where she has a working partner of sufficient experience and rank she may share that duty, and all that it entails, with him as her High Priest. However, although they run the Coven jointly, the High Priestess still takes precedence. If there is no Priestess of sufficient rank and experience, then the Coven may be run by the High Priest alone. To reduce the number of times you have to read 'High Priestess and/or High Priest', and 'she/they/he', etc, I am going to refer to the High Priestess, but you can mentally adjust this to suit your circumstances.

Generally speaking, the founder of the Coven will be the High Priestess. At first, there seems a contradiction between a non-hierarchical belief system where we are each our own Priest or Priestess and the roles of High Priestess and High Priest. But in every organization, whether it be the village flower group or a Coven, someone has to take the lead. This does not mean they are better flower growers or better Witches, but they bear the brunt of the organizational responsibility and roles.

It is very much up to the individual High Priestess to decide whether she is going to establish an autocratic Coven, where the High Priestess says 'jump' and everyone else says 'how high?', or whether she will attempt to run a democracy. The only thing I will say is that most democratic Covens soon find that giving everyone a say in everything that is done results in nothing much happening, or in such protracted discussions that what is achieved is a fraction of what is intended. Most effective High Priestesses tread the fine line between coordinating and guiding, and listening and taking into account the views of their members.

I find it easier to describe the roles of High Priestess and High Priest as the servants of the Coven. It is their task to ensure that the following is carried out, and to make the following decisions, all of which are best considered in advance:

- ✮ Purpose of the Coven
- ✮ Meeting dates, times and locations
- ✮ Clothes and jewellery
- ✮ How the Coven will finance itself
- ✮ The Rites and Rituals of the Coven
- ✮ The rules of the Coven

THE PURPOSE OF THE COVEN

As High Priestess your most important decision is the purpose of the Coven. Having taken a look at your reasons for starting a Coven you also need to look at what your Coven is going to do:

★ Are you simply a group of Witches who wish to celebrate the Sabbats and work the Esbats? Do you intend to work only to expand your own knowledge or are you prepared to work magic to help others?

★ You need to decide on what style of Craft you wish to practise: Hedgewitch, Alexandrian, Traditional, or a blend.

★ You need to decide on the profile of the Coven, whether you will be entirely secret, open in the Witchcraft and/or Pagan communities, or indeed, completely open. I would advise against the latter at least until you are well established.

★ Will you be taking on newcomers to the Craft, or are you simply looking for a band of existing Witches to work together? Take care with the latter, as poaching is frowned on by most groups.

MEETING DATES, TIMES AND LOCATIONS ARE SET, AND CLEARLY COMMUNICATED

You will need to decide how often your group is to meet. Generally speaking Covens meet at the Esbats (Full Moons) and Sabbats (8 seasonal festivals), and some groups will also meet at the New Moons. You can, if you wish, choose meeting dates by a number of criteria:

★ The most obvious is to hold the Sabbats, Esbats and, if you intend to hold them, New Moons, according to the calendar. This is no doubt the most logical method.

★ Some groups automatically default their meetings to the nearest Saturday night, as most, if not all, of their members will have travelling time before the meeting and do not have to rise early for work the next day.

★ You can, of course, set each meeting date by consensus, ie ask everyone when is convenient for them and pick the date with fewest potential absentees. This tends only to work if you have a small number of people as the larger the group the more variables come into the equation. If your group grows you may well have to change this policy.

★ I do know of at least one group who meet every second Saturday and celebrate, or work, whatever seems closest on the calendar. I feel this really isn't in the true spirit of the Craft, although it may work for them.

Whatever system you choose, try not to lose sight of the fact that group members should be prepared to make some kind of commitment to the group. The Coven is not run for the convenience of individuals, but so that those who wish to join a Coven may follow the Craft, and so learn and grow.

Whilst the responsibility for communicating meeting dates, times and location(s) lies with the High Priestess she does not have to undertake to do this personally. There is no reason why she should not either select a Coven member to remind people or, more logically, leave the responsibility to the individual group members to communicate with her. This latter is the method I prefer, as I do not feel that I am responsible for dragging the reluctant or bored along to meetings, they are responsible for finding out when those meetings are held if they have an interest in attending. It also helps to spread the cost of communication more evenly.

THE MEETING LOCATION IS FULLY PREPARED AND ALL SUPPLIES ARE READY

Firstly, you need to decide where to hold your rituals. Indoors or out?

An outdoor location needs to be:

★ **Accessible.** Not all Coven members are mountain goats, nor can everyone trek through the darkness carrying the wherewithal for an outdoor Ritual.

★ **Private,** unencumbered by large numbers of dog walkers (and the deposits they leave behind), or visiting groups of teenagers. You must also be allowed to use it; if you can get permission from the local farmer, great, but don't trespass.

★ **Safe,** no cliff edges that vanish when a cloud passes over the Moon, no hidden pot/rabbit holes, or thickets of brambles. If planning to use the seashore you will also need to check tide tables. As High Priestess you really do have the responsibility to come home with everyone you took out!

So, unless your group is fit and hardy, and your environment contains a really good private location which does not turn into a marsh in wet weather, you are going to need an indoor location, at least some of the time.

Now it is tempting to let this happen at someone else's house, perhaps because it is bigger, cleaner or has fewer children and animals in residence. However, if rituals are not held in the High Priestess' home there can be a number of draw-backs: unless the Coven has it's own complete set of Ritual tools you will either have to carry your tools backward and forward or leave some of your equipment there, meaning you don't have it available in your own home for personal use, or in one-to-one training held in your own home. You have to give the person host-ing the meetings the final veto on meeting dates, however inconvenient to you or the rest of the group. You may also find that group members tend to look to the person who hosts the Rituals as the one they should confer with. This can cut you out of the communication loop – always to be avoided.

Where rituals are to be held indoors, the Ritual room has to be cleaned and tidied, unless your home is always pristine! You are inviting the Goddess and the God to your Rituals, you do not want to invite them to a dump! Unless you live in splendid isolation, try to choose a room which cannot be overlooked or

overheard from the outside, unless you want your neighbours to know what you are up to. I find lined velvet, or faux-velvet, curtains great insulators of sound and light. Other rooms may also need attention; if members are going to put their coats in your bedroom you might want to ensure that your discarded clothing, dirty underwear, books, etc, are all put away. Alternatively, you may find that you need to remove a hundred small pieces of toddler toys so that the unobservant don't injure themselves by standing barefoot on the sharp bits! Scattered cat litter provides a similar hazard. You will need to clear your kitchen so that it is easy for Coven members to prepare their own tea and coffee unless you plan to provide waitress service. Put much loved souvenir china and valuables away too. And there will need to be at least one more loo roll than usual, clearly visible in the bathroom. Also remember to adjust the heating for your requirements: if you have 20 people performing Ritual in a small room (and I have) you will not need to heat it as much as you do for normal life; try not to cook your Witches!

In addition to a full set of the Ritual equipment you intend to use you will also need a reasonable supply of candles, incense, charcoal blocks, etc, so that you can undertake not only the actions you intend within the forthcoming Ritual but also any sudden requests for magic that may crop up.

Then there are the other consumables, eg tea, coffee, milk and sugar. You can always suggest to anyone with particular preferences to bring their own, in a clearly marked vessel. In addition you need to have sufficient washing up liquid and an obvious cloth for clearing spills. Last but not least, you need wine and cakes for the Rite of Wine and Cakes.

Again, you can delegate any of the above chores to someone else, but do make sure that they are reliable. It is not unheard of for the person bringing the least replaceable item to be the one who can't make it at the last minute. And there's nothing worse than returning from the last guest's departure to find your kitchen not only a nightmare, but totally devoid of the means to make a much needed cup of tea.

CLOTHES AND JEWELLERY

Hard on the heels of location comes the question of dress. There are a number of options and it has to be for the High Priestess to consider the question in the first place. She may choose to seek the views of other members but, once the group is established you cannot really chop and change to suit every new entrant. The options really fall into the following categories; skyclad, robed, costumed, normal clothes or a pre-arranged combination.

SKYCLAD

The arguments for and against skyclad go as follows:

* Witchcraft is a nature religion and naked is natural.
* Gerald Gardner, 'the father of modern Witchcraft', worked skyclad, therefore so should we. But Gardner was a Naturist, he did most things naked when he could.
* The Charge says 'And ye shall be naked in your Rites'. Ah, but the Charge was written by one of the founder members of Gardner's Coven and anyway naked does not have to be of body but can be of heart.
* When naked we are all the same. Well actually we are not, we don't even look the same, some are short, some tall, some fat, some thin, etc. And besides, we are all individuals with differing talents and I feel we should accept each other for what we are within and on the surface. We should not confuse equality in rank with seeking to be identical in all aspects.

★ Being naked removes marks of rank and wealth. So it may have done in the days when your clothes denoted your social status, but as we all gather together and prepare for Ritual together anyone who is hung up on marks of rank can check out their neighbours' clothes before and after the Ritual.

★ You should be naked to allow the power to flow. Hmmn, any power that cannot get through a layer of fabric has to be a bit weak!

The basic options are thus:

SKYCLAD ALL THE TIME

Some groups do work skyclad (naked) for all their Rituals, whether indoor or out. However, to work skyclad outdoors you need a really safe, secure and private location. It's no use harping on about what we should be allowed to do, if the police are called you will have a lot of unpleasantness and probably a lot of unwanted publicity. Indoors there is less of a problem, although you may find that this deters some perfectly good candidates from entering your group. And yes, you really should tell them before they pitch up in Circle and find out for themselves, for your own protection as much as for their comfort. However much you think they won't mind there is always the chance that a person will turn out to be totally insulted and offended, and may even choose to make an issue out of it, and you just don't need the grief! For those of you who feel that this is the choice you would prefer, but have that one often unspoken reservation: menstruating women who do not use internal protection are usually allowed to keep their underpants on.

SKYCLAD SOMETIMES

This may include skyclad indoors but not, or only sometimes, outside. The groups that do this are sometimes weather dependent, and yes I know it's warm when the Circle goes up, but it isn't always before or after. Not all Witches are young and fit, some have physical problems which are exacerbated by being exposed to too much cold.

Some groups hold their Initiations skyclad, but not the bulk of their Rituals. A few Covens require the Initiate to be skyclad whilst the rest of the Coven is not.

Again you will need to make sure your Covenors are aware of this, for the same reasons as above.

ROBED

Many groups work robed. That is, in special garments which are precisely or broadly similar throughout the group. Generally speaking, robes are either full length or reach to mid calf. Robes have the effect of giving the group a unity of appearance and of separating Craft working from daily life. Some Covens insist that members should be skyclad under their robes for indoor Rituals. Generally, robes are girdled at the waist with a cord, or sometimes a belt, from which can be hung an Athame (the 'witches' knife', see page 211).

Robes tend to be in dark colours for two reasons, both connected with outdoor working: firstly, dark does not show the dirt or stain so easily, and everyone should be required to keep their robes looking nice. Secondly, dark robes are less conspicuous in the dark and can even enable the wearers to vanish into the night.

Having said that, some groups have robes which are brightly coloured and even highly decorated. And it can be wonderful to see a Coven which looks like so many brightly-coloured flowers.

Some groups will actually use the cord which goes around the waist as a colour coded system to show who is at which level of initiation. If you are planning to do this then you must spell it out to newcomers who will otherwise simply select the colour they prefer.

Many who wear robes and work outdoors will also invest in a cloak, for chillier occasions.

IN OTHER 'COSTUMES'

A few groups will choose an alternate form of clothing which is reserved for magical use but would still not really be referred to as robes. Female Witches may select a special dress which becomes their magical clothing, males will often opt for a form of tabard. Occasionally, groups will choose the costume of a specific period or style which reflects an historical period.

IN NORMAL CLOTHES

Some groups simply wear their normal clothes. For outdoor working this has the advantage of everyone simply looking like a group of people who happen to be out for the evening, and, if your site is not very private, can avoid the curiosity of passers by.

FEET

Almost all Covens work barefoot indoors and a great many do so outdoors, too, in order to feel connected to the earth. If you are planning to do this outdoors you will need to ensure that the ground is reasonably flat and devoid of broken glass, bits of old iron, etc, and it may be as well to take a small first aid box with you just in case.

JEWELLERY

I have seen Witches in Circle wearing so much jewellery that when they kiss during the Rite of Wine they become inextricably locked together! I cannot but feel that anyone who feels the need to come to Circle draped with a dozen icons of the Craft, and a handful of talismans of protection, is probably in the wrong group. Once in Circle you should need no reminders that you are a Witch and certainly no charms of protection from your fellow Coven members!

To my mind jewellery falls into four main categories:

* ✷ The fancy/pretty stuff you wear to complement your outfit or just because you like it, which should be removed before Circle work. I include in this those items of jewellery that I wear specifically for the media.
* ✷ Talismans to demonstrate you are a Witch, or for healing and protection. Again you do not need these in Circle.
* ✷ Stuff you always wear and/or cannot remove. Wedding rings usually fall into this category, as do very recent piercings. Your pentacle may also be included.
* ✷ Ritual Jewellery, which is never worn outside of the Circle but is put on before commencing any kind of Magical working.

In all aspects of clothing and jewellery, there is no right and wrong way to do it. But if you want to set some kind of a standard in your group, you will have to make your decision and communicate it. It's no use simply expecting your example to be copied if you don't give your group the idea that it is supposed to be an example!

HOW THE COVEN IS FUNDED

As you can see from the above section, there are a large number of things which need to be purchased to make the Coven run effectively. The High Priestess cannot be expected to fund this out of her own pocket. Most of us can't afford it, and even if you can this is a group enterprise not an event you are putting on for your own benefit. Coven subscriptions (or subs) need to be set at a sensible level and collected regularly. Now it is up to you to decide whether to charge by the meeting or go for a less frequent collection; either way you must set a system and stick to it. One of the ways of setting the rate of Coven subs is to look at the supplies you estimate you will need for a full year, divide this figure by eight and collect that amount at every Sabbat. You can always review the amount and frequency at a later date. Our group has at various times charged by the meeting, the Sabbat, and the quarter. You also need to decide the thorny issue of whether people pay whether they attend or not; after all, they are still group members and sooner or later everyone will miss a meeting.

Coven funds can also be used for other Coven-related reasons. I have in the past given a member cash to purchase a pregnancy test and to pay for urgent veterinary treatment of a puppy. You may also wish to accumulate enough cash in the box to cover the purchase of jewellery or other group gifts, given to the Initiate at the time of Initiation. If, after a period, you find that Coven funds are seriously in credit you can always use them to pay for a really good Sabbat feast, or have a period where no subs are collected. I can't say this has ever happened to us, but you never know.

As money is one of those issues that have a great capacity for controversy it is best to keep a record of what is paid; when, and by whom, and what it has been used for. The cash itself should always be kept in a separate and secure place. It is a good idea to delegate the gathering of money and the keeping of the record, the collector always feels less embarrassed if doing it because the HPS says so! However, it is not a good idea to let the funds leave the Covenstead. If a group member loses the money it is very embarrassing for both you and them; if you lose it then you simply have to repay it! I have had a Coven member lose a significant amount of money from the Coven cash box, almost certainly lifted by either a member of his extended family or other visitor to his home. This was embarrassing for him, cast a cloud over his dealings with visitors to his home and left the Coven short of cash.

THE RITES AND RITUALS ARE PREPARED, COMMUNICATED TO, AND UNDERSTOOD BY ALL MEMBERS

Even if you are following a set book of Rituals you will still need to assign roles within each Ritual and make adjustments for those who have to cry off at the last minute. I do not believe in the handing out of lots of sheets of paper so that people can read their 'script' by candlelight (if they have good eyes) and rustle their way through the Ritual. This is not amateur dramatics it is Witchcraft and therefore it is the intent, not the precise wording, which counts. For regular roles, such as Blessing the Elements, Calling the Quarters, inviting the Goddess and the God, Casting the Circle, and the Rite of Wine and Cakes, produce a text and get members to learn the words in their own time, not in Circle. Yes, there will be some mistakes, but 'in mirth and reverence'! Other aspects of the Ritual can be more freeform and, as High Priestess you can prompt, or even make them stop and start again. They and you will soon get used to it and your group will soon develop a relaxed and confident style of their own.

What I tend to do is to write a plan of the Ritual with assigned roles and I leave this on the Altar so that members can have a look at it in preparation time. Then once we have gathered in a Circle, but before we actually start, I read this aloud and do my best to ensure that everyone knows what they are doing.

You can, of course, share the burden of writing Rituals by assigning other group members, either separately or jointly, to take a turn.

This has a number of advantages:

- ★ It gets you off the hook when it comes to devising new and interesting things to do, and is especially useful if you intend to write your own group's Rituals.
- ★ It gives members an insight into the complexity of devising a good strong Ritual which is meaningful and fun for all.
- ★ It gives you the opportunity to see if any of your members are budding prima donnas who assign all the 'interesting stuff' to themselves, and also the chance to see what they think are the 'best roles'!
- ★ It expands the skill base of the Coven and often results in new and intriguing ways for everyone to look at the Craft.

If you do decide to try this out, be prepared to check that the person is not struggling for ideas or has not forgotten the whole thing. It's no use just saying 'ask for help if you want'; people don't.

THE RULES OF THE GROUP ARE SET, AND ENFORCED

Yes, you have to have rules. However democratic you want to be, everyone needs to know where they stand. In Chapter Three, Rules and Discipline, I will look at the types of rules and the methods of keeping discipline, but be aware that you must have some rules, right from the word go.

OTHER ROLES WITHIN THE GROUP

THE HIGH PRIEST OR ACTING HIGH PRIEST

The High Priest stands alongside the High Priestess. He is her working Partner both within and without the Circle. He is equal in authority and responsibility although, should it ever become necessary, the High Priestess retains the 'casting vote'. He should support her in all Coven activities and be seen to actively uphold her authority. An effective High Priest will also be her confidant, counsellor and adviser, allowing the High Priestess a totally secure forum for discussion of her thoughts and feelings, worries and doubts about the Craft and the Coven. A good High Priest is worth his weight in gold. I know, I've got one.

Where a High Priestess has no permanent High Priest, or vice versa, you will need to address the issue of who actually takes that role in Ritual, unless of course you are running a single-sex Coven. Generally speaking, if there is a Priest of sufficient rank and experience you may wish to make him the Acting High Priest until such time as he can take the title of High Priest. However, there is one occasion when this may not work well, and that is when that Priest has an existing working partner also within the Coven. Even though all your Rites may be symbolic your need for close communication with your High Priest may cause problems within the relationship or within the Coven. In this case, or in the case of having no obvious candidate, you may wish to rotate the role through all the males. This gives all a chance to experience the role, and you the opportunity to ensure that all receive knowledge of a role you trust they will one day fill on their own behalf.

THE COVEN MAIDEN

There are traditionally a number of roles other than High Priestess and High Priest which can be assigned within the group. Probably the most contentious of these is the role of Coven Maiden. There seem to be a number of highly different interpretations of this role, not to mention a number of problems generated by each, here I will look at two extremes, and a compromise:

THE HIGH PRIESTESS IN TRAINING

This sees the Coven Maiden as the Priestess next in rank to the High Priestess. She is the High Priestess's main helper and the one to whom all manner of information necessary to run a Coven is passed.

There are a number of drawbacks to this approach:

★ The one you select may not turn out to be the next one to run their own Coven. Quite often the choice of who goes off to found a new Coven is made by the Goddess, when, for example, she arranges for the current Maiden to move to a new area for reasons apparently unrelated to the Craft.

★ Your Coven does not grow rapidly enough for the Maiden to hive off and she then spends many years being the only one to whom you are passing this information, somewhat repetitively after a while.

★ Your Maiden gets delusions of grandeur. Oh yes, they do! It's surprising how often any Coven member, let alone the Maiden, decides that the way to 'help' the High Priestess is to ensure that other members come to them with problems, ideas and so on. The next thing you know is that there is a subset of people with their own communication loop and you have little or no idea what is happening, let alone any control over the situation. This is the reason that one of the founding members of the modern Craft does not allow her Coven members to communicate whatsoever outside of groups meetings, and I can appreciate her reasons.

THE NEWEST FEMALE FIRST DEGREE
WITCH OR COVEN MEMBER

This sees the Maiden not as the confidante and successor to the High Priestess but rather as her helper in the practical realm. In this case the Maiden is the one who helps prepare the Covenstead for Rituals, and who sets the Altar. She is often given the task of ensuring that supplies and stocks of consumables are sufficient. She may also help by tending to the Coven equipment and ensuring that it is ready prior to Ritual, and cleaned and put safely away afterwards.

This role of Maiden does have the very real advantage to the occupier of the title in that she spends extra time in the company of the High Priestess at a time when she is new to the Craft and has many questions to ask and much to learn about the Craft and the Coven.

The main downside to this version of the Coven Maiden can lie in the frequency with which new members join the group: too frequent and the succession of Maidens learn little whilst giving the High Priestess the same training to do, and the same heart failure when fragile Coven effects are being handled for the first time. Too infrequent and the Maiden ceases to learn and starts to feel like a glorified skivvy! But you cannot regulate the flow of new entrants to suit the training schedule of the Coven Maiden.

ROTATE THE ROLE

A way around the difficulties of the above two forms of Coven Maiden is to rotate the office, perhaps giving each incumbent three or six months in turn. In this way all the females in the group have an opportunity to work closely with the High Priestess, and to assist her with Coven tasks and duties. The High Priestess also benefits by having a period of closeness with each and the opportunity to assess, guide and mentor in a more personal way.

THE SUMMONER

There is of course one other objection to the Coven Maiden – what is her male equivalent? Well, where the Maiden is seen as the High Priestess in training, then her male equivalent could be seen as the Summoner. He, like his title suggests, summons the Coven. He is the conduit through which the High Priestess sends details of meetings, requests for magical working and all manner of other useful information. Those of you who have been reading carefully will have already spotted the main problem! You are in effect appointing someone whose very job it is to cut you out of the communication loop. Unless you have a close relationship with the Summoner (in which case he would probably be your High Priest) he is the one through whom the group communicate.

Of course I am aware that what I have done with both the roles of Maiden and of Summoner is to give you a number of very good reasons not to appoint people to these roles. Having said that, you may choose any number of compromises. It can be very useful to rotate the Maiden through the female Coven members, perhaps changing the role twice a year. Similarly, you can ally this role to that of Summoner so that they form a pair who change regularly. Alternatively, you could

combine the roles to create the High Priestess' Second who performs both sets of duties and is likewise changed at regular intervals.

THE COUNCIL OF ELDERS

Often this is a group of people made up of the High Priestesses and High Priests of the Mother Coven and Daughter Covens. These meetings give those people the opportunity to have their own forum for communication, advice, and a much needed chance to swap horror stories about the antics of Coven members! Having said that, in a large Coven you may see the need to have a Council of Elders, simply to provide those with a lot of experience the opportunity to work without having to ensure that Aspirants or First Degrees are kept up to speed. In keeping with my insistence about staying in the communication loop, you should rarely, if ever, allow the Council to meet without your presence.

OTHER ROLES

You will find in time that your Coven members show different skills in different areas and it is a wise High Priestess who makes the most of this, for example:

THE OUTDOORS SPECIALIST

This is the person with the local knowledge, who can be relied upon to find outdoor working sites, to prepare them and, if required, to ensure there's enough wood for a good but safe working fire.

THE SHOPPER

This is that remarkable person who always knows where to find the best cheap candles, the obscure incense ingredients and moreover enjoys the search for such bargains.

THE COMPUTER WIZZ!

If you decide to have any kind of a web presence then try to find this person first. Not only can they help you get set up but, if you are very lucky, they will help you to deal with the deluge of emails that result!

THE ASTROLOGER, TAROT READER, HERBALIST, CANDLE MAKER, ETC

Not only should these people be encouraged to use their skills for the group, but to pass that knowledge on to those who seek it. Whilst I would like to be all knowing and the font of all wisdom, I know that when it comes to, say, silver-work, I as well as everyone else will benefit from the knowledge of an expert. What I tend to do every so often is to produce a checklist of as many talents and skills related, however loosely, to the Craft that I can think of. Across the page I have three columns; Can teach, Can do, Want to learn. Each group member gets a copy and ticks the boxes that apply to them, and from this I suggest group workshops where we all try to improve our knowledge.

Of course, the responsibilities of the High Priestess do not stop here. You also need to look at the finding of members, their training and development and the Rites of Initiation you wish them to go through. Those of you who are coming to this having worked in another Coven first, will probably find that you take the best bits of your own High Priestess's practice and build upon that. You will also be aware of the rewards of running an effective Coven. If you do not have that head start, you will need to make these decisions and choices for yourself, and discover the positives as you go along. As I go through this book I will try to give you enough information to help you consider all these options, and more. But one thing I would say, don't expect to get it all right immediately. All High Priestesses make mistakes, I know I do!

THREE

RULES AND DISCIPLINE

As I said in the previous chapter, you will need rules and you will need to enforce them. I know you are dealing with people who are grown up, who have made a conscious decision to become Witches and to join your Coven, but if you leave it to them to decide what they will do and when, you will have chaos! Furthermore, you will find, just as there are some people who start Covens for the wrong reasons, there are some people who join for the wrong reasons, but more of this in the next chapter. Here we are going to look at setting the regulations before you choose the people, so that you can prepare for any potential problems, and so that you can communicate those rules right from the start.

So, what rules do you select? How do you communicate them? How will you enforce them? Well, one of the main things to bear in mind is: don't ask or expect anyone to do anything you would not be prepared to do in their place.

Rules and regulations should have the following effects:

★ They put into place enough structure and order to enable the Coven to do what it was set up to do.

* They make it difficult for anyone unwittingly to fail to uphold the Craft.
* They make it difficult for anyone to hurt, harm or upset their fellow Coven members.
* They enable everyone to know where they stand and what is expected of them.
* They make the life of the High Priestess and her Covenors easier, not harder.

What they should not do is:

* Restrict people's freedom of will and ability to develop.
* Become an end in themselves.
* Become the bugbear of Covenors, or of the High Priestess.

In order to fulfil these criteria it is useful to make the rules few and simple. Do not over-elaborate or try to cover every eventuality, you'll simply tie yourself in knots! In the following section I shall suggest some rules, and explain some of the thinking behind them:

SUGGESTED RULES

Coven members will keep the secrecy of the Craft and of the Circle. This means that they do not reveal other members' names, the locations or times of Rituals to anyone outside of the Coven. They do not discuss the Craft or the Coven, even amongst themselves, in the presence of others, ie at work, in the supermarket or in the bus queue, not even if they think everyone else present is a Witch. This includes Pagan and Wiccan conferences and conventions, not

only because many attendees are not of the Craft, but also because we do not discuss details of our Coven in front of other Witches. This rule is for the protection of all, as even if every member of the group is happy to be known as a Witch, they may still not want their Sabbat gate-crashed by a bunch of people who thought it would be fun to see the Witches in action. This rule is also covered by the Coven Oath (see Chapter Five, Rites of Entry and Initiation), but needs careful and frequent reiteration, as many a Covenor has found to his or her cost that the all-Witch audience contained someone who either wasn't a Witch or who couldn't wait to report their loose tongue!

Coven members will make every effort to attend all Rituals on time. You will, if you run a Coven long enough, come across a species of Covenor who behave as though the Coven is an extension of their social life. They feel free to attend if they feel like it and nothing better comes up. I also tend to include in this category those who are too tired, hung over, etc from a previous activity to make it to meetings, or to function when they arrive, and those who are habitually late with no good reason, as well as those who turn up inconveniently early.

Coven Members are responsible for arriving in a fit state for Ritual. This is an extension of the former because you will also come across those whose Craft life comes a poor second to everything else. They fail to remember their robes, etc, or their robes look as though they've spent the period since the last Ritual rolled in a ball in a plastic bag. This also covers those who have undertaken to provide something, or learn something, for the Ritual or some other task, but have 'forgotten' or 'been too busy'. You will have few Coven members who are so busy they couldn't at least have made a phone call to explain. They should also be sober and healthy enough to take part. It may sound harsh but you, and the rest of the group, do not need to be magically supporting someone in the worst stages of flu, nor do you need the germs.

On arrival Members will settle down and prepare for Ritual. As High Priestess you

will barely have the time to do all the domestic, Ritual and personal preparation you need before Ritual. You do not need what is left of your equanimity blown by a bunch of people discussing their personal lives, other people's personal lives and the latest events in a soap opera. If you have it planned right they will arrive, change (if that is what your group does), read the Ritual to make sure they understand it and be ready to start. Something else covered in this, is the tendency of members to have urgent business to discuss with the High Priestess just as Ritual is about to start. Obviously, you are there for their real problems, but very few of these urgent matters will have cropped up on the day of Ritual, and most can wait until the business of the evening is complete so that you can let the rest of the Coven get away on time. *Members will pay Coven subs on time.* It shouldn't need spelling out but ... *Members will complete their Book of Shadows after every Ritual and will bring it with them to every meeting.* Now this rule will depend upon whether you decide that the keeping of Books of Shadows is a good idea or not. However, there are a number of very good reasons for keeping such a magical journal:

- ✮   They have a record of their magical workings, and can see what works for them. In the fullness of time they will have a full set of Rituals on which to base their own group or their own magical practice.
- ✮   You have a record of their magical workings and can see if the individual, or indeed the whole group, have problems with what you are doing.
- ✮   You get a very real idea of their commitment to the Craft. Someone who is always too busy, or can find one of a hundred 'good' reasons for not getting this done, needs, at the least, a spot of encouragement!

There are some people with very poor writing skills, or who are dyslexic. You can choose to excuse them from this task, or to reduce the amount of their input, or to excuse the quality of their input, but I would recommend one of the latter two options. Otherwise, everyone will want to try a similar excuse.

Just in case you have any doubts about what a Book of Shadows actually is and contains, it is the individual's magical journal. In it they write details of Rites, Rituals and other Craft workings. Each entry should include:

- ✬ The date and time of the Ritual and the phase of the Moon.
- ✬ The purpose of the Ritual or magical working.
- ✬ Their role within the Ritual (but not details of who else was there or who did what).
- ✬ How they felt the Ritual or working went, their feelings at the time and just after.
- ✬ Any subsequent effects of the Ritual, personal feelings, and whether the magic worked.

It is quite important that the Book of Shadows reflects the detail of workings and how the individual felt, but that it does not in any way indicate who else may have been present, just in case it gets read by the wrong person. There is more on Books of Shadows in Chapter Eight, Developing the Coven.

One of the odd things I have noticed about getting people to complete their Book of Shadows is that the more I have to get on to people to complete them, the more they thank me about 12 to 18 months down the road.

Coven members forming relationships with other group members will inform the High Priestess. As I have said elsewhere, at least one High Priestess actually forbids her members to have contact outside of the Circle. I still prefer, however much I have regretted it in the past, to avoid making this a rule. However, as High Priestess you do need to be aware of the group dynamic, and if two people have just started an intimate relationship it will have an effect on the group as a whole. You don't need all the gory details, nor do they need to make a public statement, but it is helpful to be told. It can also help you to spot the (thankfully rare) Covenor who sees the group as some kind of singles' club.

Coven members with complaints about the High Priestess or any aspect of the group, will inform the High Priestess first. In the first instance this is only good manners, but it also gives you the opportunity to sort things out before a small issue becomes a large one. It also helps to prevent the occasional trouble maker from splitting a perfectly sound group by gossip and innuendo.

This is just a selection of the rules many High Priestesses find it useful to lay down. There are many others you can add, but as I said before, it is best to resist the temptation to try to cover every possible eventuality. You tend to find that, the more precise the rules, the harder some people will actually try to get around them!

Now some of you may still feel that the laying down of rules smacks of being overly domineering, or that such rules are either over-controlling, or state the obvious. All I can do is reiterate that these are decisions that I have come to from experience. I have in fact run a Coven with no formal rules which depended on its members adhering to their Coven Oath, exhibiting adult behaviour, self-control and common sense. It was less than a year before we were sitting down, writing rules! Of course, if you wish to proceed without formal regulations, that is fine and I, and most of the High Priestesses and High Priests of my acquaintance, wish you luck. Remember, a Witch can be defined as Healer, Teacher and Parent; well, being the High Priestess certainly requires the teacher and parent qualities.

COMMUNICATING THE RULES

Obviously you cannot expect people to follow rules they are unaware of, so you need to communicate them. I favour the approach of discussing the rules with each person before they join the Coven (more of this in the next chapter) and then reiterating them on a regular basis, usually whenever a newcomer joins the group. Yes, that means the newcomer gets told twice in quick succession, but that just helps it to sink in. I have ceased to hand out copies of the rules because I find it simply represents a challenge to a minority of people.

ENFORCING THE RULES

Well, the bottom line has to be: 'If you don't like our rules you know where the door is!' Harsh, but definitely to be remembered as the last resort. Otherwise, you need to look at whether you are facing forgetfulness, misinterpretation, stupidity or spite! A person in the throes of a heady romance with another Coven member may forget they should have mentioned it to the High Priestess, although you would think that one of them might have remembered. A person who has got away with being late for the last 3 meetings, may presume you have relaxed the rule, so remember to say something, however gentle, every time. A person who has been told to look after their robes may feel that covered in mud and rolled in a ball constitutes care, so you will have to explain. But a person who deliberately ferments disruption has probably got their own agenda. In all cases you have to try to see through the excuses to the motivation, to take into account the frequency of the problem, to ascertain if they have outside problems which are affecting the situation, or whether you need to apply a heavy hand.

Before you get to this stage you will need to have, at least, a sort of mental list of punishments in mind. You do not need to be overly draconian, so start with small things: washing up for the next three Rituals, or a formal apology to every Coven member kept waiting when they were late. Try to make the punishment fit the perpetrator, as well as the crime. I have one Covenor who loves polishing the

brass-ware, so obviously no punishment for her there. However, you shouldn't put someone with a detergent allergy onto the washing up, unless you can also provide gloves. Severe punishments, such as temporary or permanent banishment from the Coven should be kept for offences which may endanger Coven members or potentially bring the Craft into disrepute, see 'Serious Problems' below.

Which brings us on to the sensitive issue of the scourge (see Chapter Five, page 72). One very well respected High Priestess once said, 'I'd have no truck with the scourge, except it works!' You have to decide whether you are prepared to wield the scourge, and what scale of scourging you think is acceptable. I strongly suggest that, if you are going to incorporate this into your Craft then you do so after discussion with other experienced Witches, and preferably with senior or founding members of your own Coven. Last, but by no means least, ask yourself, 'would I accept it?' Before my mailbox fills up with letters accusing me of being a sadist, or perverted in some way, I would point out that around 40 per cent of the Witches I have asked maintain that they would rather have the swift punishment of the scourge to a long-drawn-out process of domestic duties, or being banished, however temporarily, from a Coven and High Priestess they respect. Also, remember we are talking about the scourge, not the cat-o-nine-tails!

In all cases you have to weigh a lot of factors in the balance, and it helps to have someone to discuss the pros and cons with before coming to a decision and 'passing sentence'. If you do not have a High Priestess of your own, or a High Priest in the group then I would recommend finding someone in the Craft to whom you can talk. A technique which frequently works well, whether you have others to talk to first or not, is to discuss the problem with the offender. Invite them for a personal chat at a mutually convenient time. Tell them what they have done to upset or annoy you, for example persistent lateness. Advise them of the ramifications of the problem, e.g. other people being kept waiting and being late home, extra baby-sitting charges incurred, etc. Ask them what reason they have for this. Be careful to note the difference between a genuine reason and a sob story or excuse. Finally, ask them what punishment they would set in your shoes. Frequently, I am surprised at the severity of punishments people select for themselves, and equally frequently I tone them down to something which I find more acceptable. Wherever possible deliver your justice as swiftly as possible. You do not need to make a performance out of it for the whole group, although in some cases this has the effect of making everyone aware that you mean business. More usually you, or the offender, can report it to the whole group at the beginning of the next meeting. Lastly, make sure that the incident is completely finished with.

SERIOUS PROBLEMS

As I mentioned above, severe punishments, such as temporary or permanent banishment from the Coven, should be kept for offences which may endanger Coven members or potentially bring the Craft into disrepute.

TEMPORARY BANISHMENT

Here you are basically looking at temporary banishment for a set period, usually where someone has acted thoughtlessly or carelessly. Temporary banishment normally means not being allowed to attend group meetings, but usually requires that some form of contact is maintained with the High Priestess or her representative. The period in question is usually between 3 months and a year and a day. During the period of banishment the offender is usually encouraged to work on their own, but to refrain from contacting other group members. This period does not count towards Initiation where the group sets Initiation on a time-served basis.

Reasons for temporary banishment might include:

★ Making it possible for outsiders to locate the Coven or its members.
★ Giving away details of Craft or the Coven workings.
★ Bringing the Coven into a bad light.
★ Bringing the Craft into a bad light.
★ Putting Coven members at physical risk, perhaps by selling a fellow Covenor a known dodgy car, or by putting such huge quantities of an accelerant, such as petrol, on the fire, that it becomes positively hazardous.

If you are certain that any of these were done maliciously, perhaps because they have a grudge, or for personal gain, then you may want to look at the next option.

PERMANENT BANISHMENT

Permanent banishment, or dismissal from the Coven, should be reserved for only the most serious rule-breakers. Not only should you be thoroughly glad to see the back of the offender, but you should also be prepared to face any internal problems this may raise with the other members. A good many Covenors face the world with a huge trust of their fellow man and a redeeming zeal by which they believe everyone can be reformed! Personally, much as I would like this to be the case, experience has taught me that there are a few Covenors you are better off without, and the sooner they part from the group, the sooner the rest of you can get back to the practice of Witchcraft. In very extreme cases you may also need to warn other High Priestesses of the offender's peccadilloes!

When any form of banishment has been decided upon it is usually a good idea to hold a group discussion so that you may explain your thoughts and the other Covenors can get any issues out into the open. This is not so that they can change your mind, but so that they have a chance to understand the issue and its potential ramifications.

SQUARE PEGS AND RACEHORSES

There is one other category of person you might like to consider at this time, and that is the person who, whilst behaving reasonably, does not really fit in with the group. In this case we are not talking about any form of disciplinary issue, but about serious incompatibility. Running a Coven can be a bit like trying to harness a team of horses to a cart: the odd racehorse will not fit in! It is not that they are any worse than the others, in fact they may, in their own way, be better, but they do not fit. It is only fair, under these circumstances, to discuss the problem with them, in an unhurried way. You may find that they can also see the problem, or that they are trying to be someone or something they are not, and hence seem to be out of step. If, after every effort has been made, the incompatibility cannot be resolved, then wherever possible a High Priestess should try to see if there is another Coven that might be prepared to take them. If this is not the case then you can only offer to give them some personal support and a good reference should another High Priestess ask for one.

INTRA-COVEN STRIFE

Just occasionally you will have a situation arise where two Covenors have a serious disagreement which means they are reluctant to stand in Circle together.

If you are absolutely certain that one is the 'victim' and the other the perpetrator then you can simply refer to the above disciplines.

However, this kind of situation often occurs at the end of a relationship. In this case it is frequently best not to get embroiled in questions of who did what to whom, as both parties are likely to have highly coloured recollections of the relationship and the problems. In these circumstances it is often best to suggest both parties try a cooling-off period of Solitary work. Assign each a mentor within the Coven, preferably of their own gender, just in case! Then wait to see how the situation develops. In a good many cases a few months is all that is needed to see the resumption of adult behaviour. However, some people will never be reconciled and in these cases you may be obliged to choose which of the two Covenors you prefer to keep and which to let go. There are many criteria you can use for this, such as the letting go of the person whom you can most easily place in another group, or keeping the one with the most reliable attendance. But all other things being equal you may simply have to opt for the 'last in first out' formula. All you can do is think carefully about your actions, make your decision and stick to it.

Of course, if you wish to be really firm then you can banish both parties until such time as they can come to the Coven without bringing their personal differences with them. Unfortunately, this tends to result in two fairly poor actors pretending to have put their differences aside whilst continuing a petty sniping war. Whatever you do will be seen as unfair by at least one person, and frequently you may find that this is another situation which causes dissension within the group.

Whilst it is preferable to view the High Priestess as constantly being loved and respected by all, regrettably you cannot please all of the people all of the time. There may even be the odd time when you are neither loved nor respected, and these are the times when you have to stand firm. If your rules are clearly communicated, in advance, and justly applied without favour, then your Covenors' respect for you will grow, even though it may seem shaky at times! Of course, a lot of the problems can be avoided by having the right Covenors. Let's look at how we might find them.

FOUR

FINDING COVEN MEMBERS

So you've decided why you want to run a Coven, what sort of Coven it will be and what it will do. You've thought through some rules and what you will do if anyone doesn't follow them. Now you need some Coven members, so how do you get them?

At this point, for ease of reading, I'd just like to make a couple of definitions clear:

* ★ *Candidate* Someone who wants to join, about whom you have yet to make up your mind. Some Candidates may be Initiates where they have self-initiated, or in some cases the Initiates of other Covens. However, there are concerns attached to taking another person's Initiate which I will discuss later in this chapter.
* ★ *Aspirant* Someone who has joined the Coven and has taken their Coven Oath, but has yet to take their First Degree Initiation. These are sometimes referred to as Neophytes.
* ★ *Initiate* An Initiate of any degree, including the High Priestess.

★ *Covenor* Any member of the Coven who has taken their Coven Oath, from Aspirant to High Priestess.

ATTRACTING CANDIDATES

Regrettably the Craft attracts more than its fair share of strange people, because there are still a great many who believe that what they have read in Dennis Wheatley, Harry Potter and the more lurid newspapers, is the truth. There are also those who think it is a branch of Satanism, a series of sexual orgies, a blood cult, or any one of a number of totally unrelated practices you will want nothing to do with. Of course if these are what you are after, then you are not practising Witchcraft.

Just to give you an idea of why I am so cautious: in addition to a large number of really excellent candidates, many of whom have turned into Initiates and Witches to be proud of, I have also had the following:

★ A letter which read 'I want to join your Coven. Do you have lots of naked girls and can I take photographs?' He forgot to send an SAE, so I forgot to reply!

★ A person who wanted to redeem himself because he was the reincarnation of Matthew Hopkins, the Witchfinder General.

★ A young lass who wanted to try my Coven because none of the others would let her fly her broomstick.

★ Several requests from teenagers wanting to turn boyfriends, teachers, parents, etc., into toads.

- ★ An elderly chap with 'a secluded garden where ladies can take off their clothes'.
- ★ A seriously mentally disturbed person, who I finally managed to persuade to seek professional psychiatric care.
- ★ Several people of the 'I've tried all the other beliefs this year and thought I'd give yours a go' persuasion.
- ★ More than one person who 'just knows' Witchcraft will make them beautiful, rich, famous and irresistible to the opposite gender.
- ★ The Solitary Witch with 'decades of experience' who turned out to be 13 years old!

Even if you don't get the truly disturbed or dangerous, you don't want to spend all your energy on time wasters, so you can see that you have to be a little cautious about how you go about attracting candidates. You could stick a notice in a local shop window giving your home phone number, but I strongly recommend against it – you don't know who might crawl out of the woodwork! At the very least you might get some helpful interest from your local church, at the worst every loose screw in your neighbourhood is going to be on the line within a week. You definitely do not want to give your home or work address away. Not only are there many strange types you want to avoid, you also do not want even the most benign people just turning up for a quick chat, when they feel like it. At one time I had a very highly public profile which meant that my home address could be traced. This led to several doorstep encounters that were frequently totally inconvenient; from unwanted candidates who turn up just before Ritual is about to start, to the less premeditative people who arrived just as I was on my way out, in the bath, or had just got the baby off to sleep.

The following are some guidelines to safer ways of 'advertising':

- ★ Ask the Goddess. It's amazing how many people don't think of this most simple of steps. There is a small Rite which you can perform, even on your own if there's only you. At the Full Moon, have on your Altar, in addition to your usual equipment, a plain white candle, and put up your Circle in the normal way. Sit cross-legged in the centre of the Circle, facing North, and visualize the Goddess. Hold up the candle to her and ask her to send you candidates who will serve her well and who will be right for your Coven. Light the candle in her honour and to seal your request. Meditate on the Goddess and your Coven. When you are ready, thank the Goddess. Then take down the Circle, but let the candle burn all the way down. If you cannot do this without leaving the candle unattended, then burn it down in stages over this and the next two nights.

- ★ Get in touch with a contact group. The Children of Artemis seek to find genuine candidates for reputable Covens, and you can find their details in the section on contacts. You will still need to check these contacts out carefully, but it does mean that at least some of the loose wheels will have been eliminated.

- ★ The contacts section of a Pagan/Wiccan magazine. Whether you place a contact ad or simply reply to existing entries, choose a magazine which allows you to have a box number, and use it, even if this is an extra cost.

- ★ Join a local Pagan or Wiccan group. Here you will get to meet people from your area in neutral surroundings. You never know, after a few meetings, you may find the right people and you can take things a bit further.

- ★ Use the internet. If you have your own website or home page you can always use this as a way of seeking candidates. You can also respond to other people's postings. But please do remember the guidelines on staying safe at the end of this chapter.

FIRST CONTACT

Having got a pile of applications to join in front of you, what do you do? Well if you have a postal box number or are using email then you simply start corresponding for a bit. Here are some useful questions to ask, some Craft related, others more general:

* ✯ 'How old are you?' You may want to check this, so you can always follow up with 'I'm interested in Astrology, what's your date of birth?' It's not a guarantee, but it can help to weed out some who are not entirely truthful!
* ✯ 'How long have you been interested in the Craft?'
* ✯ 'What started your interest in the Craft?'
* ✯ 'What books have you read?'
* ✯ 'Have you ever worked in a group?'
* ✯ 'Where abouts are you?' They will almost certainly be as cautious as you about giving out their personal details. But if you live in Manchester, fascinating as it may be to continue an email discussion, someone in Lithuania is not going to be an ideal attendee of your Coven unless they own a private aircraft!
* ✯ 'Do you ever go to any Pagan/Wiccan events?' If they do, this would be a great place to meet them.
* ✯ 'What other interests do you have?' For candidates to fit into a group, it usually helps if they have some interests in common with the group. Besides, you might feel strongly about the candidate who puts 'fox hunting' or 'bull-fighting' down as their first choice.

★ 'What do you do for a living?' It helps to get a perspective on someone if you know what they do for a day job. It's also a good question, because generally people feel more comfortable talking about what they know.

There are many other questions that you can ask, simply to get to know about them a bit, questions about interests, hobbies, pets, music, TV and so on. Just be a little wary about how much 'location information' you give in return. If they know that you live in the small village of A, have long black hair and support the local band B, who play in pub C every Saturday, they are not going to find it too difficult to track you down.

PERSONAL CONTACT

Assuming that you still feel this person is a suitable candidate, sooner or later you are going to want to meet up. As I said earlier, one of the best venues for this is some kind of Pagan or Wiccan event (see Points of Contact for places to look). Here you are on neutral ground, with lots of other people, and you can talk about the Craft in general without arousing too much curiosity. Even so, I would suggest that you try to find someone you know to go with you. That way if your candidate seems a bit strange, too keen, or even just a bore, you will have someone to rescue you. Don't be put off if the next suitable event is a couple of months away, better to proceed slowly.

However, if you don't have an accessible or timely event to go to then, assuming you still want to meet them, you will need to arrange something else. The best way to proceed is to select a neutral location in a place you know well. It should be somewhere reasonably close to you and easy to travel to and from.

Choose somewhere relatively busy where you can go in the daytime. Coffee bars in shopping centres are excellent for this. Arrange the meeting to have a time limit: 'I'll be there at three, but I have another appointment at four,' so that you are not stuck there all day. Make some kind of recognition plan, and stick to it. It's no use saying you'll be in a blue jacket, if the first thing you do when you get there is take it off! Choose a seat or table in view of the door; they won't find you if you hide in a corner or behind a pillar. Take a friend along; if they are also a member of your group, fine, both of you can meet the candidate. If no other group member is available then take another friend, even if you have to ask them to keep a watchful eye on you from the next table! You can always tell them it's an internet contact. If you really must go on your own then be extra careful, let the candidate leave first, or wander around the shops until you are sure there's nothing amiss. I know it all sounds a bit 007 but better safe, huh?

It's worth pointing out that I, along with others, also give this cautionary advice to people seeking to join a Coven. They too are right to be cautious about meeting a stranger. If they have brought someone along to watch over them you might like to consider introducing yourself, especially if this is a parent, as this can often help to reassure them that you aren't about to abduct their near and dear.

If the first meeting goes well then you can have other meetings. Perhaps you could move on to invite them to a friend's party, or to some other social event. Your other friends may not be Witches but they will still have gut instincts and may well tell you if they feel something is not quite right. If you are really starting your Coven from scratch then you may find it easier to seek your first candidates from your own gender and age group, as these will be people with whom you are likely to share some common ground and about whom you are better placed to make an assessment. Once there are several of you it becomes easier to meet and assess people of all kinds.

But what is the point of all this correspondence and these meetings? Well, actually it is quite easy to find people wanting to join a Coven, but you do want

to find the right people. As I've said before, when it comes to selecting Covenors it is not a question of whether they are right or wrong for the Craft, but whether they fit in with your group.

In order to try to find this out you will need some kind of 'testing' period. This doesn't mean you are going to set them exams but rather that you are going to try to find out what sort of people they are:

★ Whether they understand what real Witchcraft is, or have ideas straight out of fiction.

★ Whether they are going to be committed to the Craft, or this is just passing curiosity.

★ Whether they will get on with everyone else.

In other words, you attempt to find out whether the Craft is right for them and they are right for the Craft, and whether the Coven is right for them and they are right for the Coven. A pretty tall order really!

This testing or trial period used to be very formal. A potential applicant would get in touch with a member of the Coven who would, if they felt them suitable, suggest them to the High Priestess. The candidate would then spend a year and a day knowing only that their first contact was, or sometimes just might be, a Witch. The candidate might meet other Coven members socially, but only knowing them as friends of their first contact, not that they were Witches. The candidate would be advised by their sponsor on things to read and do, which would help them to understand a bit more about the Craft. Towards the end of the year and a day the candidate would meet the High Priestess, without knowing her role, so that she could assess the candidate. If the candidate was then deemed acceptable they would then be invited for First Degree Initiation. It would only be during the course of that Ritual that they would experience their first real Witchcraft and learn who the other members of the Coven were.

There are still many Covens who practise this system today. However, a great many more Covens prefer a more open approach, of which the following is an example:

A potential applicant contacts the Coven, either through a Covenor, by mail, internet, or at an open meeting if the Coven holds them. Some training Covens receive applicants through the Children of Artemis who provide an introductory service (see Recommended Reading and Points of Contact at the end of this book). Where contacts are via the mail or internet, there will usually be several letters before any personal contact is made. The applicant's first meeting will almost always take place on neutral territory: a bar, cafe or similar. The High Priestess and at least one other Coven member will meet the applicant several times to talk to them about their interest in the Craft. If the candidate seems suitable they may be invited along to a Coven social event, so that several members of the group have a chance to meet them. The candidate will be recommended to read some books and perhaps to try some exercises from them. The only real difference thus far, between the old system and the newer one, is that the candidate is aware that they are being seen and probably assessed by members of a Coven. Generally speaking, after a few months the candidate may be invited to other Coven events, possibly even to an 'open Ritual' if the group holds them.

So, during the course of your meetings you will be trying to find out what the candidate expects of the Craft; what they already know about it and whether they are prepared to learn; their attitude towards the Goddess and the whole concept of a High Priestess, and their likely commitment to the Craft.

THINGS TO BE WARY OF

Obviously, there are many personal habits and characteristics which you may find off-putting, some universally disliked and some which just upset or annoy you. But these are some of the less obvious things that you might like to keep an eye on:

★ The candidate is frequently late. The candidate should be the one who is most keen! If they can't make it to these meetings, are they likely to be on time for the Coven?

★ The candidate never finishes any of the suggested reading you gave them. You may need to, tactfully, find out if they have a reading problem. Suggest something off the fiction list at the back of this book or even something unrelated to the Craft. However, if they can manage light fiction, why not a book on the Craft?

   By the way, this is a good place to mention that it is not a good idea to lend your books to candidates, or indeed to pretty much anyone whose home you are not prepared to go to in order to retrieve them, just in case!

★ The candidate frequently interrupts or talks over you. I'm not suggesting you want active worship from them, but manners would be nice.

★ The candidate knows best. Whatever you are telling them, they can always go one better. In the early stages this could be nerves or a desire to show their knowledge, but if it happens every time, it's going to become, at the very least, extremely wearing.

★ The candidate touches all the time. Even if you come from a tactile background, you need to be wary of a near stranger who is always touching you. In some people it indicates a desire to control.

- ✭ The candidate invades your personal space. This can also indicate a controlling personality.
- ✭ The candidate is always looking around or over your head. If someone is interested in you and what you are saying they will look at your face. Not only is it irritating to have someone with wandering eyes, it can also mean they're on the look out for the more interesting option.
- ✭ The candidate tries to borrow money from you. Don't! Again, if they have respect for the Craft and for you as a Priestess, they wouldn't dream of it.
- ✭ The candidate makes derogatory comments about people around you, or about other people's beliefs. You have to ask yourself whether they have so many redeeming features that you can put up with their lack of respect for the rest of the world.
- ✭ The candidate makes you feel uneasy. You can't put your finger on it but they make you feel uncomfortable. You can, if you wish, give them the benefit of the doubt by meeting a couple more times in a neutral place. But ultimately you should trust your instincts, that's what they're there for!

There is one other category of potential Candidate you need to be cautious of, and that is personal friends of yourself or of one of your Covenors. It is essential that you assess a person as an individual, not because of your affection for them, or because they are the partner, relative or close friend of an existing Initiate. In these cases you need to make it abundantly clear to the person who introduces them, as well as to the candidate, that your assessment has to be made for the good of the Coven. It can be very hard to turn away someone's partner, and may also result in the loss of a 'good' Covenor, but you owe it to yourself to be firm.

After several meetings, and usually a few months, you may decide that you feel this person is suitable to consider as an Aspirant. At this point you will need to have a rather more formal discussion with them.

FROM CANDIDATE TO ASPIRANT

Assuming your candidate has successfully passed all these hurdles and you feel they would be a useful addition to your Coven, you will need to give the candidate a more formal interview which explains, very clearly, what would be required of them should they be allowed to join the Coven. This interview is not all one-sided as you the High Priestess will also do your very best to ensure that the candidate has no illusions about the Craft and to answer their questions as fully as possible. In my Coven this is known, semi-humorously, as the Riot Act because when given to a candidate it is information, but if I have reason to repeat it to experienced Covenors then they're in trouble! If the candidate is still keen, and you feel they are right for the group, then you can make arrangements for them to take their Coven Oath.

SIZE IS IMPORTANT

It is very tempting when starting a Coven to think that big is beautiful and that you want lots of newcomers. But this is rarely the best move. A small number of people can become close and in harmony far faster than a large number of newcomers, most of whom are largely unknown to you.

In an ideal world a Coven may probably consist of:

- ✴ A High Priestess and High Priest and possibly one or two other Third Degree Witches just about ready to start their own group.
- ✴ Several Second Degree Witches, some recently 'made up', others with some experience.
- ✴ Several First Degree Witches, of various terms of standing.
- ✴ A few Aspirants, moving towards taking their First Degree.
- ✴ A few candidates moving through their pre-entry testing period.

This gives a fair spread of experience and the potential for a through flow of new-comers, right up to those who are ready to hive off. Whilst the traditional number of 13 Witches to a Coven is largely invented, it is not a bad rule of thumb if you have a fair scattering of experience. The trouble comes if you have one High Priestess, one other Initiate and 6 or so Aspirants, all of whom need and deserve a lot of time spent on them.

TAKING ON THOSE ALREADY INITIATED

As mentioned above, 'poaching', the attracting away of someone else's Covenors, is very much frowned upon. Think how you would feel, if having spent months or years checking someone is suitable and training them, another High Priestess entices them away.

Most of your candidates will not be initiated. However, every so often you will be approached by someone who is an Initiate. This can be for a number of reasons, some good, some more worrying:

✯ The candidate is a self Initiate. Here you have no problem, there is no High Priestess or initiator to consider. It is up to you, but I, and most other High Priestesses will treat them as any other candidate, including the careful assessment, Aspirant and Initiatory stages.

✯ The candidate is changing Coven with the blessing of their previous High Priestess, and helps you to contact her. In which case do contact her, not only is it the polite thing to do, but you will also be able to find out more about this newcomer to your group. And you get the chance to communicate with another High Priestess. You will probably want to put them on a probationary period, but once you are happy that they will fit in, you can allow them to continue their Craft from their stated level of development. If, however, this person is a Third Degree High Priest you may wish to re-celebrate the Third Degree in order to keep continuity in your line of Initiation.

✯ The candidate says they are leaving with the consent of their previous High Priestess but that she is not contactable for some reason. I would view this with a certain amount of suspicion, after all, High Priestesses are usually very nice, helpful people, aren't we? The candidate may have nothing to hide, but! In this case I would do my best to make some enquiries around the Craft, see if anyone has heard of this person, or of their High Priestess. If this turns up nothing then you may like to consider treating them as you would any other new candidate, or if your instincts are alerted then you do not have to accept them. Do not let them try to push you into a corner by referring to the Oaths of Initiation. They are referring to 'I will never deny the secrets (of the Craft) to such a person (one properly prepared) if she or he has been properly vouched for by a brother or sister of the Art.' The pertinent phrase word is 'properly vouched for'. If you have taken these oaths you are not under any obligation to take someone who tells you that they have been initiated by an uncontactable, and possibly even unnamed, High Priestess. They have not been 'properly' vouched for. Indeed to do so would violate a different oath: 'I will never reveal the secrets of the Circle, unless it be to a proper person.'

However, if you have taken these oaths, it does mean that, should a brother or sister of the art 'properly vouch for' a candidate, you are under an obligation to take that person on. Or at the very least to assess them and come up with a really good reason why they should not become part of your group.

★ Occasionally you may get a candidate who states that their High Priestess has died, or moved out of contact, in which case, unless the Coven has disbanded, someone should have moved up to take her place. Make your enquiries as before.

★ The last category of Initiate seeking to be a candidate is quite rare, but nevertheless you may come across one. This is the candidate who has been permanently banished from their old Coven. Logically, you would be justified in having nothing to do with them. But I would just like to stress that the final decision is yours. You can, if you wish, make the same enquiries as before, or you can start them at the very beginning of the process. Whatever you decide, remember to use your instincts for each and every candidate.

There is one other concern you need to be aware of when considering someone from another Coven: because their first experience of the Craft will have been with someone else, they will always be tempted to compare you, and your techniques, with their previous High Priestess. This is not a problem if they are prepared to keep this to themselves, or to share any questions and comments with you alone. However, if they are going to bring this commentary into your group, you are going to need to be very firm. It is one thing to share Craft experience, it is quite another to allow it to interfere with the working of the group. At the very least, constant references to the previous Coven will become quite tiresome, in a worse case you may find their enthusiasm, coupled with a likely absence of any negative comments, causes your other group members to think this other Coven must in some way be better. This can be very divisive.

STAYING SAFE

Whatever the technique you use to make contact with candidates, there are some guidelines which never change:

★ Never give anyone your surname, home, college, or work address, until you are absolutely certain they are trustworthy. About the time you have decided to let them take their Coven Oath, for example.

★ Never give out your mobile or home telephone number, until you have verified their contact details. Get them to give you their number and ensure that it really is their number by ringing them. Make your first calls from a call box, use 141 or some other way of screening your number until you are certain they can be trusted. This will also help you avoid anyone who feels that, having been given your number, they can call you at any and every occasion.

★ Always arrange first (preferably second and third) meetings on neutral ground, which is local and known to you. Meet in the daytime, in a place where there are plenty of other people about.

★ Always try to take someone you know and trust to first meetings, even if you get them to watch over you from a short distance away.

★ Never go off with someone to a quiet place. If they need to get something from their car to show you, you can wait where you are until they get back.

★ Don't give away too much personal information.

★ Always have the ability to get home under your own power.

★ If you can, set up a postal box number for letters and contacts. It's not that expensive and you may only need it for a few months anyway.

★ If you are uncertain for any reason, back out.

FIVE

RITES OF ENTRY AND INITIATION

You have attracted and assessed your candidates and chosen those you feel will make a contribution to the Craft and to your Coven. You have interviewed them and prepared them to take the first steps on the path of the Witch. In this chapter we are going to look at the initiatory system from Coven Oath through to Third Degree. I have included substantial parts of the First and Second Degree Initiation Rituals, but please be aware that these are not entirely complete. The Third I have only outlined. Generally speaking, the full details of the Rituals of Initiation are kept secret because to put them entirely into the public domain would be to allow pre-initiates and those who are not yet ready, to read them. A huge part of every step in the initiatory process is the trust with which you enter the Circle to face that which is unknown to you. If I detail it here then the pre-initiate who reads it will not be able to demonstrate that trust, as they will know what lies ahead. Purists within the Craft may find that these Rituals are not those they recall, or practise, but the Craft is not a stale belief system and should change and develop over time.

I will, however, be looking at some of the meanings behind these Rituals, and some of the aspects that go into them, as well as where they fit into our path within the Craft. This should, even if you have no heritage of your own, enable you to effect meaningful Initiations, once you have grasped the principles of the Craft.

THE INITIATORY SYSTEM

As mentioned in the previous chapter, it used to be traditional for the candidate to wait a year and a day before knowingly meeting the Coven and experiencing Ritual. That first meeting would take place at his or her First Degree Initiation. After that the new Initiate would take their first steps in really learning the Craft. Sometime after that, at least a year and a day, but frequently longer, the First Degree Initiate would take their Second Degree Initiation. A further period along the way they would then take their Third and final Initiation. There are branches of the Craft who still pursue this system, and there are also others with other systems; only 2 initiations, only 1 initiation, more than 3 initiations, and so on.

However, a system which is becoming more popular these days is roughly as follows:

The candidate is selected as in the previous chapter, through a process which usually takes 6 to 9 months. After this they take their Coven Oath and become an Aspirant and Covenor. This enables them to take part in some, but not necessarily all, of the Rituals and meetings of the group. I say 'take part' because I expect them to do so, I do not believe that anyone can really gain much from just observing. At least a year and a day after their first meeting with the High Priestess the Aspirant takes their First Degree. Either a year and a day, or sometimes 2 years after taking their First Degree, they take the second. Finally, again

after either a year and a day, or 3 years, they take their third. The decision between these two sets of dates, or the choice of any other, is entirely personal to the Coven concerned. In all cases it is up to the High Priestess to determine that the person is ready for whichever stage of Initiation is being proposed. Hence the time periods mentioned should be considered guidelines, not absolute. I have known of Witches who have waited 5 years to move from first to second and even as long as 20 years to move from second to third.

In the Craft, Initiation is passed from female to male and from male to female, reflecting the balance between the Goddess and the God, and that required within the Craft. The two parties are referred to as Initiate and Initiator. There is a third role necessary, that of sponsor, that is the person who brings the Initiate to the Circle and vouches for them. Thus in the Initiation of a male Witch, the Priestess is the Initiator and a Priest is the 'sponsor', and for a female the roles are reversed. Where Initiation takes place within a Partnership with no supporting Coven, or where only Initiator and Initiate are of sufficient rank to participate, the Initiator will also be the Sponsor.

In most Covens the High Priestess and High Priest are usually the Initiator and Sponsor, although there can be exceptions to this, for example, when the Initiate has a partner of appropriate rank who is able and willing to take on that role. In general, a Third Degree can Initiate to First, Second or Third Degree, whereas a Second Degree can only Initiate to First. Some traditions allow a female First Degree to Initiate a male to First, and a female Second to Initiate a male to Second. Very few Covens practise this in reverse, however.

Where a Coven does not have a Priestess or Priest who can be the Initiator, it is usual for them to approach another Coven for the 'loan' of an Initiator of the appropriate gender. It is part of the Oath of the Second and Third Degrees that they cannot refuse the Craft to a 'proper person, properly prepared and properly vouched for by a brother or sister of the Art'. In this day, when it is relatively simple to locate members of the Craft, and to stay in regular contact, the excuse of not being able to find an Initiator of the opposite gender is only valid in the most extreme of circumstances. An Initiation between people of the same gender (who do not fulfil the exceptions mentioned below) is likely to be looked at somewhat archly by other members of the Craft. Nor is the excuse of not being able to find an Initiator in time a valid one, because if the Goddess does not facilitate this, perhaps she has her reasons! An Initiator approached in this way must be prepared to accept responsibility for their Initiate's development, and will need to take steps to ensure that this responsibility is carried out. Having said that, usually the person who vouches for the potential Initiate will be a Third Degree, with no partner of sufficient rank of their own, and therefore capable of carrying out the Initiate's training and development.

The only exceptions to the male/female line of Initiation is for a mother to Initiate her daughter, or where the Coven is a dedicated single sex Coven, as in the Dianic tradition.

But what are these steps in the Initiatory process? Well, firstly I would say that in each case the Initiate is making promises to the Goddess and the God, and seeking their aid and support in the Initiate's path through the Craft. The High Priestess and the Coven are there to facilitate and mark these steps and, in the Third, to pass on power. First, I will give you a simple outline, then we can look at each step in turn.

In simple terms the steps are as follows:

The Coven Oath A promise made by the Candidate which is designed to remind them to maintain the necessary secrecy of the Craft and the Coven.
The First Degree The Aspirant's statement of beginning to learn and walk the Path of the Witch. Here they start to learn.
The Second Degree The Initiate is considered ready to take the next step, that of learning to teach.
The Third Degree The Initiate is ready to start their own Coven, when the circumstances are right.

SOME CORRESPONDENCES TO THE LEVELS OF INITIATION

The Three Degrees of Initiation also link, or correspond with many other aspects of the Craft, just a few of which are given here:

First Degree The New Moon, the Maiden aspect, youth and enthusiasm, knowledge of life, knowledge and understanding of the self, beginning to learn.

Second Degree The Full Moon, the Mother aspect, maturity and fruitfulness, knowledge of death, knowledge and understanding of others, learning to teach.

Third Degree The Old and Dark of the Moon, the Crone aspect, age and wisdom, understanding of the cycles of life, death and rebirth, combining the knowledge and understanding of self and others, teaching to learn more oneself for as we teach so we learn.

THE COVEN OATH

If you intend to let your candidate(s) experience something of the work of the Coven as part of their assessment period and prior to any Initiation, then it is a good idea to provide some formal entrance to the group as well as a way of ensuring that they understand the requirements of the Coven, especially regarding secrecy. The Coven Oath allows you to mark this as a formal entry to the Coven and to reinforce the concepts you wish them to take on board. Broadly speaking, the Coven Oath is a simple statement, taken either in the Circle, or just before the

candidate's first Circle. It should be emphasized that this is the Candidate's promise, made on their honour, to the Goddess and the God, and that neither the High Priestess nor the Coven has any power to enforce this, other than by asking the person to leave the Coven.

In my Coven we usually hold the Rite of the Coven Oath at one of the minor Sabbats of Yule, Oestara, Litha or Madron. The reason for not holding it as a stand-alone Ritual is to enable the new Aspirant to actually take part in Ritual immediately following acceptance by the Coven. The reason for it being a minor Sabbat, rather than a major one is because these are celebrations rather than working Rituals and should the Candidate change their mind at the last minute, it will not disrupt a major event. The wording and meaning of the Oath will have been explained in detail to the Candidate before they come to the Circle. It is performed with the whole group standing in Circle. After the Elements have been summoned and the Goddess and God invited, the Candidate will be called to kneel before the Altar and will repeat the words after the High Priestess:

'I (Candidate's name) undertake this Oath of my own free will, in the presence of the Old Gods and before all here present:

'I will not reveal the secrets of the Craft, nor use the knowledge I gain to impress the foolish, nor to frighten the childish. I will follow the Old ways, in humility and obedience, to the best of my ability, and uphold the Craft as best I may. I will not reveal the secrets of the Circle; the nature or detail of it's workings, nor the names of it's members.

'As I do will, so mote it be. Blessed Be.'

The group will, as is usual, echo the *'Blessed be'*.

After they have given the Oath they are an Aspirant and will be greeted by each of the other Covenors in turn. The rest of the Sabbat Ritual will then take place as usual.

I usually explain the essential components of the Coven Oath in something of the following way:

 'I (Candidate's name) undertake this Oath of my own free will, in the presence of the Old Gods and before all here present.'
The Oath is made to the Goddess and the God, and this promise is witnessed by everyone there, including the Elements. The Oath is made on the personal honour of the person taking it. The High Priestess and Covenors do not in any way have a hold over the person, although they may, however, decide to ban them from the Coven should the Oath be broken.

 'I will not reveal the secrets of the Craft,'
The Aspirant does not talk about the Craft to anyone. I extend this to include other Coven members, unless they are actually in a Coven meeting at the Covenstead, as it's surprising what can be overheard!

 'nor use the knowledge I gain to impress the foolish, nor to frighten the childish.'
They will not use the Craft, or magic, to impress or scare people. This also includes, but is not limited to, leaving books on the Craft 'accidentally' on display, covering the walls with occult symbols, having a fully set up Altar where it can be seen by visitors, wearing huge and ostentatious pentagrams, etc.

 'I will follow the Old ways, in humility and obedience, to the best of my ability,'
They will follow the tenets of the Craft; especially the Wiccan Rede and the direction of the High Priestess, to the best of their ability. This means not just following the words but their spirit also.

★ *'and uphold the Craft as best I may.'*
This means not bringing the Craft into disrepute, not running down the Craft and, where it is possible, defending the Craft. It does not mean you have to 'come out' or in any way jeopardize yourself or your family in defence of the Craft.

★ *'I will not reveal the secrets of the Circle; the nature or detail of it's workings, nor the names of it's members.'*
The Circle is the Coven or group, and this means that the Aspirant will not tell anyone the names of group members, where or when the Coven meets, or has met, nor what it does, whether inside or outside of meetings.

★ *'As I do will, so mote it be.'*
Here you are stating that you wish and intend to keep this promise and are asking the Goddess and the God to support you.

★ *'Blessed Be.'*
This means what it says literally, be blessed, and is said at the end of many of the statements made in the Craft. It is echoed by the rest of the group to indicate they also mean this.

After the Coven Oath the Aspirant is granted access to some but not all of the Rituals and meetings of the group. This is still a trial period, but one which gives the High Priestess and the group a chance to assess the Aspirant in Circle as well as outside. It also gives the Aspirant a chance to see Circle working and to get an idea of whether this really is the path, and Coven, for them. In my group I would expect the Aspirant to attend at least one minor Sabbat and perhaps a low-key Esbat, in addition to a couple of meetings where there is no Ritual. At one time we held all our minor Sabbats as 'open Rituals' where Aspirants might be invited to participate.

INITIATION

Assuming all has gone well with the introductory process, there will come a point when the High Priestess considers that the Aspirant is ready for Initiation. It used to be said that the would-be Initiate should ask for Initiation. However, in practice this rarely works, as most 'good' candidates or Aspirants are aware that they need to convince the High Priestess that they are ready for Initiation, and are then too modest or shy to actually ask. As a result you will find that you often need to prompt the question! Of course, there are always some very keen individuals, who have read all the books, and who will pester you from the moment they have known you for a year and a day. Don't let yourself be driven to initiate anyone who you don't feel is ready to take the step.

There are several points to be taken into consideration when deciding whether a person is ready or not:

★ Are you sure the person is truly interested in the Craft, for what it actually is, rather than for any fictional representation?

★ Are you happy that they will fit in with your group? However well intentioned they might be, you want to try to avoid anyone who will 'rock the boat'.

★ Do you feel comfortable with them as a person? A vague feeling of discomfort is often your inner mind's way of telling you to be cautious. Generally speaking you should trust your instincts on this.

★ Many Witches believe that a Karmic bond is created between Initiate and Initiator, whereby the Initiator accepts responsibility for the magical workings of the Initiate, from First Degree until they resume personal responsibility in this area when they are given their Third Degree. Whilst it is sometimes also believed that this bond can, in certain circumstances, be severed, you do need to consider whether you are sure enough about the Aspirant to make this commitment.

If you are uncertain, you can always extend the Aspirant stage, or simply explain that you do not feel that they will fit in with your group. Over the years most of my Aspirants have turned out to be worthwhile, but a few have caused significant problems. The problematic ones have most often been those about whom I felt a vague discomfort, but could not find a 'real reason' for not allowing them entry. As a result I tend to be more aware of my instincts, even though I might appear to be somewhat arbitrary in my decisions. It's worth mentioning here that none of us will get away with no mistakes, we just have to try to minimize them.

PREPARATION FOR INITIATION RITUALS

The Initiator and any other Covenors taking part should be familiar with the words and actions required during the Ritual. This is partly for the comfort of those participants, but serves the primary function of giving your Initiate a seamless Ritual. Initiations are scary enough, for even the most blasé of Initiates, without having ominous pauses accompanied by furtive muttering because you find your-self in the wrong part of the Circle, or without an essential piece of equipment.

Initiators can also find Initiations quite nerve-wracking. To mitigate this, where we have enough people, we have an extra role in the Circle, that of script holder or 'prompt'. This person carries a book with the script, printed in a large, easily-read font. Their role is to ensure that they are always standing close to the

current speaker(s) and can point to the exact place in the words should anyone forget where they are.

If you have not done many Initiations of this level, or if it has been a while since your last one, then it is a good idea to have a practice run. This can take the form of simply talking through the 'script', or you might prefer to have a full rehearsal of the words and actions. You may feel confident that you can remember everything, but it's surprising which odd detail(s) you forget when the time actually comes.

Prior to any Initiation Ritual the Aspirant or Initiate should have fasted for at least 6 hours, unless there are medical reasons why this period should be shorter. You might also like to insist that they have drunk nothing other than water or milk for 24 hours, to free the body of all stimulants such as caffeine, etc. Immediately before the Ritual they should wash their hair and bathe, using no cosmetics, lotions, unguents, etc. They should also remove all jewellery, including sigils of the Craft, although you may have to allow any rings which cannot be physically removed! Some Covens prefer the Aspirant to bathe at the Covenstead, others find that the size of their home means that it is impossible to do this and keep the Aspirant separate from the other Covenors.

THE FIRST DEGREE

The First Degree Initiation marks a person's formal entry to the Craft. The Ritual should be attended by all the Initiates of the Coven, but never by anyone who has not been Initiated.

In addition to your usual Altar equipment you will need:

1 x 9 foot and 2 x 4 foot 6 in lengths of red cord, for binding the Aspirant.

1 fine white cord 9 feet in length, for the measure.

Anointing oil. Make your own by blending the following essential oils in 5 ml of base oil: 2 drops Jasmine, 2 drops Frankincense, 1 drop Orange, 1 drop Rosemary.

A full set of working tools, including the scourge. The scourge has a short handle to which are attached several fine cords or ribbons. It is a symbolic whip which is intended to represent the sorrows of life.

A bell. I find the best results are gained if you remove the clapper from a handbell and then strike it with an Athame (see Chapter Six, page 107) the required number of times. This stops any unwanted sounds when handling the bell.

When the Aspirant arrives at the Covenstead they are not permitted to meet the other attendees, but are kept separate and are prepared. If you intend them to bathe at the Covenstead then, unless you have a separate toilet and bathroom, ensure that no-one else needs to answer the 'call of nature'. If they are to be skyclad, as is usual, then this is the time for them to remove all their clothes, jewellery, etc. Bind them and blindfold them, and leave them sitting, not standing, as the disorientation of the blindfold could bring on a faint if standing. They should be instructed to meditate on why they seek Initiation and upon the Goddess and the God.

The traditional method of binding the Aspirant requires three red cords, as above. The long cord is used to tie the wrists behind the back with the centre of the cord, the ends are then brought over the shoulders and knotted loosely in front, in such a fashion that the Aspirant cannot strangle themselves! One of the short cords is knotted around the right ankle, the other just above the left knee.

Unless the location is warm, it is a good idea to wrap a cloak or blanket around their shoulders to prevent them getting too chilled. Initiations are, and should be, ordeals, but that is no reason to risk making them ill. This is the last chance for the Initiator to give any words of advice and guidance they feel appropriate. I usually make a point of telling the Initiate that whilst blindfolded they must allow themselves to be guided and led at all times, they must not step out on their own initiative. This is to prevent them walking into walls, doors, etc, or from stepping on the cat! The other Covenors should be getting themselves and the Altar ready, if they have not already done so.

There is an example of creating Sacred Space in Chapter Six, on page 109. It is usual, especially for the First Degree, to take your time over this, to give the Aspirant plenty of time to reflect on the step they are about to take, and to build up a fine set of nerves!

THE RITUAL

The Initiator opens a doorway in the Circle and the Sponsor leaves to collect the Aspirant. The doorway is closed, and the Coven waits in silence. The Sponsor brings the Aspirant to the doorway, guiding them from behind, usually with their hands upon the Aspirant's shoulders. En route to the Circle the Aspirant should be gently disorientated to increase the feeling of going from the mundane world to that of the Craft. We achieve this by making them walk a circuitous route, sometimes going in and out of a room more than once. You can also turn them around several times, so that they cannot tell which direction they are going.

At the edge of the Circle the Aspirant and Sponsor halt.

Initiator	*'Who stands at the gateway of the Circle?'*
Sponsor	*'Here stands (Initiate's name), seeking Initiation to the First Degree.'*
Initiator	*'Who stands for this person?'*
Sponsor	*'I (sponsor's Witch name or name), Witch and Priest(ess) of the Third (or Second, if that be the case) Degree.'*
Initiator	*'Have they been properly prepared?'*
Sponsor	*'On my honour as a Witch I vouch that they have.'*

The Initiator challenges the Aspirant, saying:

'O thou who standest on the threshold between the world of man and the domain of the Old Gods hast thou the courage to make the assay?' Then, placing the point of their Athame to the Aspirant's neck: *'Better you should fall upon this blade than enter this Circle with fear in your heart.'*

Aspirant   *'I have two passwords, Perfect Love and Perfect Trust.'*

Initiator   *'All who have such are welcome, I give thee a third to pass through this dread door.'* Kisses the Aspirant on each cheek.

The Initiator hands the sponsor their Athame, goes behind the Aspirant and pushes them gently into the Circle. The Sponsor closes the gateway in the Circle and returns the Athame to the Initiator. The Aspirant is then presented to each of the quarters in turn.

Initiator   *'Take head ye Lords of the East (South, West and North), that (Aspirant's name) here presented is properly prepared to be initiated as Priest(ess) and Witch.'*

The handbell is rung 3 times and the Aspirant is led to stand before the Altar. The Initiator then gives the Aspirant the Fivefold Blessing:

Initiator   *'In other religions the postulant kneels while the Priest towers above him. But in the Craft we are taught to be humble and we kneel to welcome him and say: Blessed Be thy feet* (kisses right foot then left), *that have brought thee in these ways. Blessed Be thy knees* (kisses right knee then left), *that shall kneel at the Sacred Altar. Blessed Be thy womb* (where the Aspirant is female)/*phallus* (for a male), (kiss the lower belly), *which brings forth the life of man. Blessed Be thy breasts* (kisses right then left), *formed in strength and in beauty. Blessed be thy lips* (kiss once on lips), *that shall utter the Sacred Names. Blessed Be.*

*'Now we shall take your measure, that thou shalt be
known to us and to the Old Gods for all time.'*

The Sponsor takes the fine cord from the Altar and measures the
Aspirant around the head and ties a knot in the cord, around the chest
and ties another knot. Lastly with the help of the Initiator, the
Sponsor measures the Aspirant from head to toe and ties a final knot.
During this process they say *'These are the measurements of your body
in life, so that in death your shroud and coffin will be fit.'* The cord is
then placed on the Altar.

Initiator   *'Before thou are fully sworn, art thou ready to pass
                           through the ordeal and be purified?'*

Aspirant replies.

There are a number of ordeals which you may choose to put the Aspirant
through, and as High Priestess you can select one or several, or add variations of
your own. Please remember that this is intended to emphasize the meaning and
solemnity of this step, it's not an excuse to vent the frustrations of the last day,
week, month, etc. Nor is it an excuse to terrorize your Aspirant!

★ A series of light symbolic lashes with the scourge, usually administered with
the Aspirant kneeling and the number of strokes being indicated by the
ringing of the bell. The traditional number is 3, 7, 9 and 21 lashes. The
Initiate should feel the scourge, not be marked by it. To get it right, practise
on your own leg in advance and then err on the side of caution.

★ Pushing the Aspirant from person to person and questioning their ability to
keep the secrets of the Craft, their willingness to learn, their potential conduct
as a Witch and so on.

✮ Splashing them with very cold water and even some flecks of melted wax, again practise on yourself first.

✮ Asking searching questions about why they wish to enter the Circle and become a Witch.

✮ Some traditions used to prick the Initiate and place a drop of their blood onto the measure. These days this really is unnecessarily risky, both for the Initiate and for you.

Once the ordeal(s) is over the Aspirant is made to kneel before the Altar.

Initiator   *'Thou hast bravely passed the test. Art thou ready to swear that thou wilt always be true to the Art?'*

Aspirant replies.

Initiator   *'Art thou always ready to help, protect and defend thy brothers and sisters of the Art?'*

Aspirant answers.

Initiator   *'I hereby sign thee with the Triple sign, I consecrate thee with oil.'* Anoints the Aspirant with oil on the belly, right breast and left breast. *'I anoint thee with wine.'* Anoints with wine. *'I anoint thee with my lips.'* Anoints with kisses.

The Initiate is unbound and the blindfold is removed.

Initiator   *'I hereby salute thee* (name of Initiate) (kisses on each cheek) *in the name of the Old Gods, newly made Priest(ess) and Witch.*
'Art thou ready to take the Oath?'

Aspirant answers.

Initiator   *'Then repeat after me* (please note, it is a good idea to read this line by line and let the Initiate repeat each line after you):
I (Initiate's name), *duly consecrated Witch and Priest(ess), here in the presence of the Old Gods, do, of my own free will and accord most solemnly swear; that I will keep secret and never reveal the secrets of the Art, except it be to a proper person properly prepared, within a circle such as I am in now. And that I will never deny the secrets to such a person, if he or she has been properly prepared and vouched for by a brother or sister of the Art. I swear that I will not use the Craft to impress the foolish or to frighten the childish, and that I will uphold the Craft in health or sickness, weary or bright, in dark days and light days til I reach the Summerlands. All this I swear by my hopes of a future life, mindful that my measure has been taken and that my weapons will be turned against me, if I break this my solemn oath. Blessed Be.'*

The Initiator now takes the Initiate around and presents them to each of the Quarters: *'Hear ye Lords of the East (South, West, North), (Initiate's name) is now consecrated Priest(ess), Witch and child of the Goddess.'*

The Ritual now pauses whilst the Initiate is welcomed by everyone in the Circle.

The Initiator presents the Initiate with each of the working tools. It simplifies the process if the Initiator takes the tool from the Altar, hands it to the Initiate whilst explaining its purpose, then the Sponsor takes it from the Initiate and replaces it on the Altar. The tools you should have are: Sword, Athame, Boline, Wand, Chalice, Pentacle, Censer of Incense, Cords and Scourge (even if you do not use it). The scourge is symbolic of suffering and its presentation is usually accompanied by the statement and question:

'For it is written that to learn one must suffer and be purified. Art thou ready to suffer to learn?'

To which the Initiate should answer in the affirmative.

If you choose to give the Initiate a gift, perhaps the sigil of the First Degree, this is now the time to do so. If, however, your Covenors are very generous and wish to each give a small present and/or a card, then it is better to wait until the feasting commences to avoid a pile of wrapping paper and envelopes covering the floor.

Some Covens now pause and allow the Initiate to consecrate their own Athame, if they have one and have not already done so.

The High Priestess and High Priest now perform the Rite of Wine and Cakes, see Chapter Six, page 96. The Initiate should stand to the left of the High Priestess so that they are the first Covenor to whom the Chalice is handed after consecration.

The Circle is now removed. It is usual for an Initiation to be followed by a feast, and many groups like to take photographs, either of the robed participants or once everyone has returned to their ordinary clothes. I probably have the 'privilege' of being the only High Priestess to nearly incinerate herself at this point in

the proceedings. So keen was I to get the smiling group in frame, that I backed into a quarter light and set fire to my hair, only being alerted by the horrified faces in the viewfinder!

THE AFTERMATH

Some Initiates feel an immediate change, others take a few days or even weeks to feel a difference after their Initiation. A few profess to feeling no different, but nevertheless a change is noticed by others in the group, and sometimes by those around them. These changes can take many forms, such as increased confidence, poise, or even a more cheerful outlook and are mostly harmless, but the ones which the High Priestess needs to be wary of include:

* ✦ A desire to share this wonderful new-found path with other people. Some Initiates can make the most ardent born-again non-smoker seem positively shy in comparison, and have to have their evangelizing zeal severely reined in! You will need to remind them that we are a non-proselytizing religion, and that they have taken an oath not to reveal the secrets of the Craft or the Coven. If you find yourself with someone who you think might be feeling this way, it is a good idea to spend some extra time with them so that they can expound their joy and wonder within the Coven rather than outside of it.
* ✦ A desire to work magic for everything and everyone, which can go as far as a sudden belief that they, the new Initiate, are the most powerful magician since, well, you name it! Just after the Initiation Ritual it is a good idea to remind the Initiate that, should they wish to work magic on their own, they must talk to you, their High Priestess, first. Not because you wish to prevent them working, but so that you can guide them as to the better techniques and the more practical approaches. Also, if they know of something or someone in

need of magical attention then you can add your support and energy to this. If this doesn't quell their exuberant enthusiasm then you will have to put your foot down in no uncertain terms, before it turns into over-confidence or indeed arrogance.

★ An over-fondness for their Initiator. It doesn't happen often, but when it does you will know it! If, for any reason, you feel that the Initiator is going to be disturbed by this, try to ensure that meetings between Initiate and Initiator are accompanied, at least until the glow wears off.

THE SECOND DEGREE

The purpose of the Second Degree Initiation is to mark the Initiate's personal growth and increased ability within the Craft. It marks the point at which you feel

they are ready to take on more responsibility and to commence passing on their knowledge to others. There are a number of approaches to this Rite of Passage, but the one we prefer in our Covens reflects those legends of the Goddess which reflect the elements of life, death and rebirth. A significant part of the following Ritual represents the Initiate's own journey to the realm of Death. For this you will need to assign a number of people to play the roles of Portal Keepers (referred to in the text of the Ritual as PK1, PK2, etc) and of Death. This journey commences on the arrival of the Initiate at the Covenstead where they are met by a senior Covenor who plays the role of the first Portal Keeper. Where you do not have enough Witches of Second Degree or above then you may need to assign this role to the Initiator, and double up on subsequent roles.

In the period approaching the Ritual the Initiate should be encouraged to read and reflect on these legends and their inner meanings, and also to meditate upon how this is reflected in everyday life. Close attention to the legends will enable the Initiate to answer the questions of the Portal Keepers and Death during the first part of the Ritual.

Some Covens work this Ritual with everyone skyclad, others with only the Initiate skyclad, yet others prefer to provide the Initiate with a special 'Initiation Robe'. This represents the garment that the Initiate wears when they meet Death. As such it is better that it is loose fitting, made of coarse cloth and roughly finished. Something like a knee-length shift is ideal.

In addition to the usual Altar and Ritual equipment you will need:

A hooded robe or cloak for the first Portal Keeper to wear. Ideally this should completely cover them and mask their identity. Subsequent Portal Keepers and Death should stay out of sight until the Initiate has been blindfolded. Blindfold.

A cup or glass with some strong-tasting liquid. This should not be the same as the Chalice. The drink need not necessarily be pleasant, but should not actually be toxic!

Initiation Robe, if used.

Anointing unguent, which you can make yourself. Take a teaspoonful of petroleum jelly and add the following essential oils: 4 drops Lavender, 2 drops Frankincense, 1 drop Myrrh, 1 drop Clary Sage.

The script of a guided visualization of the Descent of the Goddess.

As in the First Degree the Initiate should be kept apart from the other Covenors until they actually enter the Circle. Ideally they will be the last to arrive and will commence the Ritual literally on the doorstep.

The Initiate is met at the entrance to the Covenstead by the first Portal Keeper who commences the Initiate's preparation. Key to this preparation is the Initiate's ability to answer the questions to the satisfaction of each Portal Keeper, Death and the Initiator. This means giving honest answers as the Initiator will, by this point, have a good idea of the Initiate's personality and actions in the Craft and will have communicated to the others the answers he or she deems acceptable. If you have insufficient Witches of Second and Third Degree to take all these roles, then you can have individuals taking multiple roles.

Whilst the Initiate is being prepared the remainder of the Covenors present will prepare the Altar and create the Sacred Space, taking care to invite the Goddess in her Aspect of Crone and the God in his aspect of the Hunter. Although the Initiator may not be playing a role, they may wish to step in to the preparatory area to hear the Initiate's answers. Note that each Portal Keeper should go to the Circle as soon as they have completed their allotted role. In order to prevent multiple opening and closing of a gateway in the Circle it is a good idea to hold off actually Casting the Circle until the sixth Portal Keeper arrives.

THE RITUAL

PK1	*'Who are you?'*
Initiate	*'I am (Initiate's name), Witch, Priest(ess) and child of the Goddess.'*
PK1	*'Why do you come here?'*
Initiate	*'I seek Initiation to the Second Degree.'*
PK1	*'By what right do you seek such?'*
Initiate	*'I come by right of Initiation to the First Degree.'*
PK1	*'How do you come?'*
Initiate	*'Freely, by my own will and accord.'*
PK1	*'Then enter the underworld and begin your descent, for this is but the first of seven portals which you must pass, before you attain that which you seek. Do you have the courage to make this journey?'*

Initiate answers.

PK1 then admits the Initiate into the Covenstead, blindfolds them and leads them to the next portal.

Note: Where you have limited space you may have to select one or two points in a room and lead the Initiate to and from them in order to increase the perception of distance in the 'journey', or you may choose to lead them from room to room, even into the garden. Also spinning a person around, or leading them backwards and forwards, can add significantly to their disorientation and the impact of the rite.

PK2   *'I am the keeper of the second portal and I challenge you.*
Do you have the strength to make this journey, for the
weak will surely wither and fade away?'

Initiate answers.

PK2   *'You may only succeed by your own strength of will. If you*
wish to continue you must remove all sigils of protection
and all other finery, for it has no place here.'

Initiate removes all jewellery, including Craft symbols and talismans, and then is disoriented.

PK3   *'I am the keeper of the third portal and I challenge you.*
What have you given of yourself to the Craft?'

Initiate answers.

PK3   *'If you would continue then you must go barefoot along a*
path of thorns, for the way you seek is hard and beset with
difficulties.'

Initiate removes footwear and is disoriented (if you wish to simulate a path of thorns, scatter a little clean cat litter in their path).

PK4   *'I am the keeper of the fourth portal and I challenge you.*
Do you believe that you can succeed upon a quest that
many fail, for with failure may come madness and
despair?'

Initiate answers.

PK4 hands the Initiate the cup or glass mentioned above. *'Then take this cup and drink, but be aware that it contains a powerful potion that brings madness and incomprehension to those who are not ready, and having partaken of this you pass the point of no return.'*

Initiate drinks and is disoriented.

PK5   *'I am the keeper of the fifth portal and I challenge you. Are you prepared to be changed? For this journey will change you and your perceptions, and you will never again be the same as you are now.'*

Initiate answers.

PK5   *'Then cast off your outer garments for you must leave all that you are behind you.'*

Initiate removes outer garments and is disoriented.

PK6   *'I am the keeper of the sixth portal and I challenge you. I believe that you are selfish and unworthy, and fear to look upon Death. What say you to Death?'*

Initiate answers.

PK6   *'None may come before Death unless they are naked and bowed, remove all that remains to you.'*

Initiate removes remaining garments and is again disoriented.

The Initiate remains temporarily skyclad, even if you do intend to use an Initiation Robe.

Death   *'I am the keeper of the seventh and final portal and I challenge you.* (Puts Athame to Initiate's breast.) *Do you have the passwords, for if not then this blade shall end you here and for all time?'*

Initiate answers.

Death   *'Kneel before me for I am Death, the keeper of the dark realms, I hold the secrets that you seek, if you have the wisdom, the courage, the strength and compassion to pass the tests of the underworld. Do you have these qualities?'*

Initiate kneels and answers.

Death   *'I recognize you as a Witch of the First Degree and bid thee welcome to my realm. Are you willing to accept the Death of the body, of the mind and of the spirit?'*

Initiate answers.

Death now hands the Initiation Robe to the Initiate, who puts it on. Where the Initiator has also been present to observe the Initiate's responses, they will return to the Circle at this point.

Death	*'I anoint thee with an unguent that will give your spirit flight to face the dangers and to accept the knowledge of the spirit realms.'*

Anoints the Initiate on the wrists, ankles and temples with the unguent.

'I bind thy body for the sacrificial altar, where your lifeblood may be spilled to attain the blessings of the Old Ones.'

The Initiate is bound with the 9-foot cord in the same way as for the First Degree, but the two shorter cords are not used.

'I shall lead you to the temple of the Crone where your faith will be tested and where you will be judged to be suitable, or not.'

Death leads the Initiate to the Circle, which has been prepared and where everyone is waiting. The Initiator waits on the edge of the Circle for Death and the Initiate to arrive.

Initiator	*'Identify yourself so that all present may know you.'*
Death	*'I am (Witch name), Witch of the Third Degree and stand here as Death. I have one here who seeks to journey in the realms of the underworld.'*
Initiator	*'By what right do they seek entry?'*
Death	*'By right of the First Degree and the courage to make the assay'.*
Initiator	*'Are they properly prepared?'*
Death	*'By my word, honour and all that I hold true.'*

| Initiator | *'Then both be welcome.'* |

The Initiator opens a gateway in the Circle and then kisses Death as they enter. Death then leads the Initiate into the Circle. The Initiator then closes the gateway.

Death disorients the Initiate and makes them kneel facing one of the Quarters.

| High Priestess | *'Behold here you find the Dark Mother, the Lady of the darkest night, Keeper of all that men shun and cower from in the light. Death is my servant and if you wish to seek me you must first suffer the pain of death, the fear of death and cross the abyss. If you have the substance to pass the tests of the elements, then you may enter my realm and seek my wisdom. Are you prepared?'* |

Initiate answers.

| Initiator | *'A sigil is marked upon you. Greet the element it signifies with its proper name and ask its blessing upon you.'* |

Inscribes invoking Pentagram of the appropriate element upon the Initiate's back.

Initiate answers.

The Initiate is made to rise, led around the Circle and made to kneel before a different Quarter. The question is repeated and the Initiate should answer. This process continues until the Initiate has visited and identified each Quarter in turn. The High Priestess may

also wish to add, or substitute, other tests in the same way as was
done for the First Degree.

Initiator   *'You have borne the tests of the elements, but now you*
             must face the final and greatest test, the test of the spirit.
             Do you believe you are worthy?'

Initiate answers.

The Initiate is untied (but the blindfold is left on), and lain across the
Circle with their head to the North.

The High Priestess reads the Second Degree Pathworking.

After the Pathworking the Initiate is made to kneel in the centre of
the Circle and receives each, or a smaller selection, of the working
tools. The Initiate must identify and describe the use of each.

The Initiator raises the Initiate to their feet and says:

             'Before you seek that which you attain, you must answer
             one last question: If granted the Second Degree what will
             you do with it?'

Initiate answers.

Assuming each test is passed, the Initiate is then sworn to the oath
of the Second Degree, and is anointed with oil, wine and kisses in the
sigil of the Second. Now the blindfold is removed and the Initiate is
greeted by the High Priestess, and everyone else in the group. As
before, if any token of this degree is to be given, now is the time.

Some Covens will hold a Rite of Naming at this point. See 'Witch
Names' later in this chapter on page 97.

The Rite of Wine and Cakes is then conducted by the High Priestess and the High Priest with the Initiate being the first to receive the Chalice as in the First Degree Initiation.

The Sacred Space is now removed and a celebratory feast held.

THE AFTERMATH

Whereas the First Degree Initiation worries the Initiate because they are not sure what to expect, the Second Degree Initiation concerns them as to whether they will pass the tests and answer the questions satisfactorily. Here we are examining knowledge, rather than simply trust, and they know it! As a result the Initiate, whilst outwardly maintaining an air of confidence, is often more nervous before the Second than they were before the First. Correspondingly, their feelings after the Ritual are sometimes more extreme too. Hence many High Priestesses like to immediately assign them an Aspirant, or newly-made First Degree, to instruct in one or more areas of the Craft, in order to give some immediate purpose and structure to this step.

THE THIRD DEGREE

The Third Degree Initiation is given when the High Priestess considers that the Initiate is ready to take on the responsibility of running a Coven. It is not, however, to be inferred or assumed that this means that they know everything! None of us in the Craft ever stops learning, in fact the more you learn, the more you become aware of what there is still to learn.

THE RITUAL

As I said above, I am not giving the text for this Ritual, as it should not be read by anyone who is not already a Third Degree Witch. As High Priestess you should be more than able to create this yourself. There are some published Third Degree Rituals, a few in whole, more in part, but if you want to maintain the secrecy of this Ritual you will need to alter those anyway. If, however, you do feel you need help or advice with this then you can always contact me through the publishers or via my website, details of which are at the end of this book.

The key points of the Third Degree Initiation are the Great Rite, the Anointing of the Initiate, the Willing of Power, the Giving of the Secret Names of the Goddess and the God, and the Rite of Wine and Cakes. Other aspects are a matter of choice for the High Priestess.

Unlike the First and Second Degree Initiations there is no reason for the Initiate to wait to avoid meeting the other Covenors who will be attending, as these can only be of the Third Degree anyway. Not only can the Initiate be present when the Circle is created, but they can take an active part in this. You might even feel it is more meaningful if the Initiate creates the Sacred Space for this Ritual.

The High Priestess can also decide whether she wishes the Initiate to undergo any tests or ordeals. Although you may feel that creating the Sacred Space single-handedly under the watchful eyes of the High Priestess and other Third Degree Witches is an ordeal in itself!

You may wish to arrange for the rest of the Coven to join you after the Ritual for the celebration. In this day of mobile phones they can always meet up in a nearby bar or similar and await your signal.

THE GREAT RITE

The Great Rite itself is the union of the Goddess and the God. To perform this the Priest invokes (or draws down) the Goddess into the Priestess and then she invokes the God into the Priest. Thus they represent the female and male aspects of the divine in person. These invocations each include the Five-Fold kiss as detailed in the First Degree Ritual. There is then a choice of three ways of performing the act of union:

✭ *The Great Rite Actual*, where the union is sexual. These days this is rare unless Initiate and Initiator are already partners.

✭ *The Great Rite in Token*, where the parties are skyclad and one lays over the other, sometimes separated by a cloth.

✭ *The Great Rite Symbolic*, where the union is performed using the Chalice and Athame as in the Rite of Wine and Cakes. This is by far the most frequently performed. This is not just a form of modern prudery as some suggest, but a sensible way of avoiding a number of potential problems. These days we are aware of the risks of Aids, HIV, Hepatitis, Herpes, Chlamidia, and other sexually transmitted diseases, some of which do not even require penetration to be contagious and can be unknown even to the sufferer. It is not simply a question of whether you trust the person in Circle with you, but do you trust any partners they may have had, and/or all medical treatment they may have received both here and overseas, over the last 10 years or even longer? There is also the question of the feelings of any non-Witch partner of the Initiate or Initiator. There have been cases of perfectly good relationships being put under extreme stress because the partner of the would-be Initiate does not want to interfere with their spiritual path, but nor do they like the idea of the Great Rite in Token, let alone Actual. Sometimes they cannot even bring themselves to ask.

Whichever form of the Great Rite is chosen, everyone but the Initiate and Initiator will have left the Circle for this part of the Ritual, and for the Anointing, after which they will return.

ANOINTING THE INITIATE

After the Great Rite, the Initiate is anointed in the symbol of the Third Degree with water, wine and kisses. After this the rest of attendees to the Ritual are invited to return.

WILLING OF POWER

The Initiate kneels and the Initiator places one hand on the head of the Initiate, the other under their right knee. If, like me, you are a bit on the short side, you will need your Initiate to kneel back on their heels! The Initiator focuses all their energy, and calling upon the power of the divine which was invoked into them, focuses and directs that power into the Initiate. With that energy also comes knowledge and instinct for the Craft.

GIVING THE SECRET NAMES OF
THE GODDESS AND THE GOD

The Initiator then whispers the secret name of the Goddess and that of the God into the ear of the Initiate.

THE RITE OF WINE AND CAKES

Initiator and Initiate then perform the Rite of Wine and Cakes, with the Initiator's partner being the one who receives the Chalice first. Any gifts can be presented at this point, after which the Sacred Space is removed as usual, and the celebration can commence.

THE AFTERMATH

The Third Degree Initiation marks the High Priestess's acknowledgement that the Initiate is ready to run their own Coven. In ideal circumstances, the newly-created High Priestess will be able to establish her own Coven straightaway. This is called Hiving off and the group thus formed is termed a 'Daughter Coven'. She takes, with the agreement of her High Priestess, a few of the people from the 'Mother Coven', in order that the Daughter Coven has some foundation. Of course, life is not always that simple, and you may have to consider whether you are going to hold back the Third Degree Initiation until you are in a position to ensure that the newly-created High Priestess can have such a foundation to work from. The alternative is to give the Third when the Initiate is ready and then have more than one High Priestess in the Mother Coven. Generally speaking, the Initiate is entitled to call themselves a High Priest or High Priestess as appropriate. However, if they are remaining within the Mother Coven it can be less confusing if they wait before using this title. As with the Second, it is a good idea to formally increase the responsibility of the newly-made Third. Where it is possible to start the Daughter Coven straightaway it is important that the new High Priestess is given autonomy to run this her own way, whilst assuring her that help and support is available if wanted.

WITCH NAMES

It is believed that in times of persecution, the new Witch would take, or be given, a Witch name. This meant that Coven members would know one another by different identities from their public names, and hence be unable, or at least less likely, to give one another away. Today this is not really necessary. However, many Witches like to take a Witch name for use within the Circle. In some Covens the Witch chooses their own name, in others the name is chosen for them by the High Priestess. As with many things in the Craft, the timing of this Rite of Naming can vary. Some Covens will include it in the First Degree Initiation, others will place it in the Second, as indicated above. Yet others will incorporate it into an Esbat or even hold a separate Ritual.

The choosing of a Witch name is an interesting process, as this name should accompany the Witch throughout his or her Craft-life thereafter. There are no particular rules about what you choose to call yourself, or others, but there are some points that you might like to bear in mind:

* It is generally felt that only the most presumptuous, or arrogant, will choose the name of a major divinity.
* Names of minor divinities, or those selected from history, legend or mythology, should be carefully researched in case there are some less than pleasant or unintended associations.
* Over-complex names should also be considered carefully; 'Silver Moonlight River Walker' might sum up your feelings about your place in the Craft, but it's a mouthful to be used regularly in Circle!
* Some names are becoming somewhat oversubscribed. There are, for example, huge numbers of Morrigans and Merlins in the Craft today.

You can make the Rite of Naming as simple or as complex as you wish. Basically, the Circle should be created as usual and the Witch to be named should be called to stand, or kneel, before the High Priestess and the Altar. The High Priestess then either asks them whether they wish to take a new name, or tells them that she is going to give them a new name, depending on whether you feel this should be optional or not. The Witch is either asked what name they will take, or told what name they are given. The Witch is then presented to each of the Quarters, and to the Goddess and the God, by their new name. Lastly, everyone else present should welcome them, using their new name.

OTHER ASPECTS OF BEING THE INITIATOR

As mentioned above, Initiation Rituals can be as nerve-wracking for the Initiator as for the Initiate. It is, after all, an important Ritual that you want to get right for your Initiate. To make the process more worrisome, Initiations are usually not something you do all that often, so it is easy to forget some of the finer details of the Rites. So here are a few hints which may help you to ensure all goes well.

✴ *Review and update.* As your Craft develops, so do you. So it is not unreasonable to suppose you may want to change the Rituals to reflect this. You may also want to put in changes which reflect the number and experience of other attendees, giving them larger roles as they grow in experience. New ideas can frequently be added to the Rituals, so it is a good idea, every so often, to review their length before they become unwieldy. Another factor which can prompt changes has been alluded to above: small Initiators faced with tall Initiates sometimes need to plan for this in the Ritual!

⭐ *Rehearse and practise.* At the very least read through the script whilst visualizing the actions. This helps to iron out practical details and can often result in you spotting potential hiccups before they happen. Personally, I like to rehearse the words and movements together with my High Priest the day before an Initiation, just to have the Ritual fresh in our minds.

⭐ *Use a script and perhaps a prompter.* For most Rituals I find that the use of pieces of paper in the Circle are a distraction and hinder, rather than help, focus, meaning and intent. However, for Initiations a complete script, in a large typeface, can be a real boon. Not only does it help you remember the words and actions, but it helps you to pace the Ritual. If you are familiar with the Ritual, you can leave it on the Altar, but at least it's there if you do need it.

⭐ *Take it slowly.* Initiations of all Rituals should proceed at a measured pace, partly to heighten the sensations of the Initiate and partly to remain in keeping with the solemnity of the occasion. There is also a practical reason, as during those parts of the Ritual where the Initiate is blindfolded, they need to be encouraged to move slowly and carefully, so that they do not injure themselves.

⭐ *Space them out.* Initiations done properly take a lot of energy from the Initiator. Even if all your Aspirants joined the Coven at the same time, try to spread out the Initiations so that there is at least a month between them. This way you will not end up draining yourself of all your energy. You may find that the Initiates who have to wait longer complain that this is unfair, but you are the High Priestess and it is ultimately your decision. Besides, if they make a fuss perhaps they are not as ready as they would like to think they are! Tempting as it may be, never do more than one Initiation on one occasion. Not only is it exhausting for the Initiator, but it will almost certainly mean a lot of hanging around for one or more people. Also, neither of the Initiates really gets the same level of attention as they would if they were done on separate occasions. The only exception to this might be where you have a

female Initiate to Third Degree who is then going to Initiate her partner to the same level, within the same Circle, so that they may perform the Great Rite Actual together. If this is the case then you will need to review the Ritual so as to minimize the amount of repetition and delay that might occur.

★ *Remember who's in charge!* One good thing about Initiation Rituals is that each person experiences each Ritual only once, unless there are really exceptional circumstances. Thus, if you the High Priestess say this is how it should be, with sufficient authority and conviction, then no-one else will have any reason to think otherwise. As my music teacher once said to me: 'If you make a mistake when you play in the orchestra, you will know and the conductor might know, but everyone else will be oblivious unless you give the game away!'

One footnote on the subject of Initiations goes to the Initiates. Whilst we do not charge for teaching the Craft, it is worth remembering that your High Priestess will have put much time and effort into your development, not to mention the Rituals themselves. Some Initiates, and most Initiators, feel that this is worth some kind of reward! Of course, one of the best rewards you can give your High Priestess is to ultimately run your own, effective, Coven. However, in the meantime perhaps some token of appreciation should be considered. I am not suggesting that you should rush out and purchase the most expensive gift you can find, although if you can afford it, fair enough. But a small token of thanks is appropriate, some flowers, a bottle of wine, or, if you are short of cash, perhaps you could help out around the home or provide some other practical aid which demonstrates your gratitude.

SIX

ESBATS AND WORKING RITUALS

Generally speaking Full Moon Rituals, or Esbats, are the working Rituals. This is the time when the Coven gathers together to work magic for each other, for their near and dear, for those who have requested it, and/or for the world at large. In this chapter I am going to give an introduction to working Rituals, and in the next I shall be looking briefly at Sabbat Rituals. Those of you who would like more Rituals and Spells will need to wait for my next book *The Real Witches' Book of Spells and Rituals*.

INDOORS OR OUT?

It is wonderful to be able to go outside and actually feel the presence of the land, the elements and nature at first hand. In the right location you can really sense the presence of the Goddess and the God. A lucky few have access to a large

secluded garden, not overlooked by the neighbours. However, it is not always as easy as that. In order to work Ritual outside you have to consider a number of points:

★ *Are you allowed?* Do not trespass. Getting picked up by the police and having to answer a number of embarrassing questions, and possibly attracting the attention of the local press, is a good way of bringing the Craft into disrepute. Besides, how would you feel if a bunch of Christians climbed over your fence to hold their Sunday service?

★ *Will you be undisturbed?* The trouble with public land is that it is public, and can be used by anyone. If there are enough of you, then you may feel that being seen by the occasional dog walker is not a problem. However, you might find you feel differently about a group of people bearing beer cans who decide to watch and heckle! Not to mention the fact that some well-meaning passer-by may decide to call the police anyway.

★ *Can everyone get there?* One of the best outdoor sites I ever came across was great if you were young and very fit, but hopeless for anyone without the characteristics of a mountain goat!

★ *Is it safe?* You must check out your site in daylight. Look for hidden rabbit holes, concealed cliff edges, broken bottles and bits of rusty wire. OK, in this day of mobile phones you can always summon the emergency services, but do you really want to have to? It is considered very poor Witchcraft to come home with fewer Covenors than you set out with! And remember, many sites can become treacherous in, or after, wet weather.

★ *Weather forecast?* It is always a good idea to check the weather forecast, and to consider working some weather magic in advance of the Ritual. Additionally, you might like to remind whoever is calling the Quarters that they should be focussed on the essence of the elements rather than on a dramatic practical demonstration. More than once I have seen the calling of Water followed by an immediate downpour!

★ *Will you leave it as you found it?* If you want to have a fire you must be careful to ensure that it does not set fire to either trees, including overhanging branches, or the undergrowth. But have you also considered that you should not scorch either the grass or the earth. To do so will certainly not bring the approval of the Goddess and the God. This means that you need either a proper fire pit or a cauldron to keep the fire in, and a good quantity of water to ensure that every last spark and ember is extinguished. Not only that, but you should also make sure that no candles or spilt wax are left behind, nor any other litter. This includes 'offerings'. In particular, please do not leave any bits and pieces, even flowers, at ancient sites or standing stones, etc. Your single daisy may seem just a small thing, but multiplied by the thousands who visit such sites it can be the start of a mountain of dead flowers. When using an outdoor location we usually take an empty bin bag which we fill, not only with our own litter, but with any other rubbish we find around the site, with the intention of leaving the place in a better state than when we found it.

INDOOR RITUALS

Here you are on safer ground, as the only real concerns are:

★ Have you, or can you create, enough space. This is where having at least one person come a little early can help, so that you can shift furniture together.

★ Can you minimize disruption to the rest of the family. I do know one High Priestess whose husband and children are content to stick to the upstairs rooms of their house for the duration of Rituals, but not everyone will have

such an amenable family. Consider how you would feel if banished to the bedroom for one or two evenings a month.

★ Can you be discreet enough to prevent the neighbours having to complain about the noise? This is where you might have to lower your expectations in terms of really boisterous chanting and drumming, etc. I'm not saying you have to be silent, but remember how you feel on the occasions when they have a noisy evening. Also ensure that your Covenors are considerate when arriving and leaving, don't block all the available car parking in your street, or have a departure which sounds like a raid on a night club!

STEPS IN A WORKING RITUAL

Whether you are working at the Full Moon or have decided that you need to work at any other phase of the Moon's cycle there are a number of steps you need to take. And whilst there are many opinions on what precisely should happen at the Esbat the following gives a good guide as to the content of a Ritual.

DECIDING WHAT TO DO

There is no point in having a Ritual unless you have a purpose. Having said that, there are very few people who, given a few minutes thought, cannot come up with the name of at least one person who needs healing, confidence for an interview, or magical aid in some area of their life. Both you and your Covenors should feel able to contribute names and ideas for magical work, and, if necessary prioritize them.

PREPARING THE PEOPLE

In order for an Esbat to work you have to have the right people, in the right place, at the right time. In a well-run Coven your Covenors will have checked with you, the High Priestess, as to when and where they should be. In the real world, you will probably have to remind one or more of them a day or so before the event!

The next important thing is to ensure that everyone is in agreement about what you will be doing. Anyone who does not agree with the nature of the magic to be performed will hinder, if not actually prevent, it from working.

Lastly, you should ensure that everyone knows what they will be doing and how to do it. It is a good idea to ensure that everyone has a part to play, and that roles are rotated around the group to increase everyone's ability and confidence.

PREPARING THE AREA

The area you will be using should be large enough for the number of people you expect to be present and should be clear and free from obstacles and hazards. If indoors, it should also be clean and free from distractions. When you create the Sacred Space you will be inviting the Goddess and the God, and you do not want to invite them to a dump!

SETTING THE ALTAR

An Altar is simply a table or other surface onto which you will place all the tools and equipment you will be using in the Ritual. Some High Priestesses have a special piece of furniture for this, but most of us use a table, or the surface of a low

cupboard. Ideally your Altar should be of a height which means you do not have to bend or stoop to reach things, nor do you have to stretch. I prefer to set the Altar in the North of the Circle, the point of power. It can equally validly be placed in the centre of the Circle, enabling you to use the whole circumference for people to stand. It could be set to the North East, the point of entry, or even to East, the starting point of the Circle, which is also the quarter of Air which represents thought, which should precede all action.

As with many things in the Craft there are differences in opinion as to what should be on the Altar. I prefer the approach of placing only what is to be used, rather than putting every piece of Ritual equipment on it, but it is a matter of choice and of available space. The following is a selection of likely Altar equipment:

★ *Altar Cloth* It is usual to have some kind of Altar cloth. Not only does this signify the change in use for your table, but it protects it from spilt wax, etc.

★ *Symbols of the Goddess and the God* Many Covens will place images of the Goddess and the God on the Altar. These may be finely wrought statuettes or items to represent them. This is definitely a case where if you can craft your own, they will have more meaning than shop-bought ones. Some groups will simply use candles for this purpose.

★ *Pentacle* The five-pointed star within a Circle is a symbol of the Craft and also of the element of earth. A flat Altar pentacle is also used as a surface on which to work some kinds of magic.

★ *Incense* This represents the element of Air. You can use incense cones, sticks or loose incense. Whichever you choose you will need a suitable heatproof container to stand your incense in. In the case of loose incense you will also need self-igniting charcoal and, of course, matches or some other means of lighting it. Many people find that a pair of sugar tongs are a safe way of holding the charcoal whilst lighting it. Do make sure that your incense burner, or thurible, is ready to hand to take the charcoal once it has sparked, as it gets very hot very quickly!

★ *Candle(s)* Candles represent the element of Fire, and the Goddess and the God. Some High Priestesses will have one candle for each of these purposes, others prefer to have just one or two candles on the Altar.

　　If you choose to use Quarter Lights, that is a candle placed at each quarter of the Circle to represent each element, usually in the elemental colours, then you may also wish to place the one representing Earth on the Altar, if it is placed in the North.

★ *Water* A bowl or dish of water represents the element of Water.

★ *Salt* Salt is used to represent the element of Earth.

★ *Wine* Wine in a Chalice will be used in the Rite of Wine and Cakes, where it represents the Goddess. Generally, a full-bodied red wine is used, but there are occasions when you might choose to use a sweet white wine or mead, although these are more likely to be for Sabbats than Esbats. Try to remember to uncork the wine at least 2 hours before the start of the Ritual, as it definitely does improve the taste. For those who prefer not to have alcohol in the Circle, then grape juice is an ideal alternative.

★ *Cakes* There is much discussion as to what are the correct kind of cakes to use. Purists prefer them to be home baked and made of only three ingredients, usually flour, sugar and butter. Have a look at *The Real Witches' Kitchen* for recipes for Esbat biscuits. However, there is no reason why you should not use shop-bought cookies although I would recommend that you keep them small so that the Circle is not held up waiting for everyone to finish theirs. As an alternative to biscuits you can always use slices of apple, a traditional Witches' fruit.

★ *Athame* The Athame is the Witches' knife or blade. Traditionally, it is a simple black-handled knife with a double-edged blade some 9 inches long. However, many Witches use Athames made of wood, bone, and other materials. The Athame is an extension of the Witch's hand, and is used to direct power or energy as well as to summon and invoke the Elements. Each Athame is

special to its owner and it is very bad manners to handle another Witch's Athame without his or her express permission. In some traditions the Athame is placed on the Altar. However, I find that it is more convenient to have it in a sheath attached to my belt. Not only is it then with me wherever I am in Circle, but it avoids the problem of having up to 20 Athames crowding the Altar!

✺ *Sword* If you choose to use a sword to actually cast your Circle, then you will need it either on the Altar, or laid on the floor just in front, in which case, if barefoot, watch out for your toes! However, there is no reason why you shouldn't cast a perfectly good Circle with your Athame, or with your finger, as it is your energy which does the work, the tool is just the focus. The sword is considered in some groups to represent fire and in others to represent air.

✺ *Wand* The wand is considered to be the instrument with which you conjure things for which the Athame is unsuitable. In some traditions this includes the elements of Air and Water.

✺ *Cords* Cords are used in the Rituals of Initiation, in which case they will be attached to the Initiate, and also to perform cord magics. Cords also represent self-restraint and self-control.

✺ *Scourge* The scourge is a very contentious tool. It is most often used in Initiation, but it also represents submission to authority. In some Covens it is used as a punishment. Those of you who are squeamish about this might like to be aware that, as mentioned before, given the choice, many Witches prefer the scourge to any kind of long-drawn-out punishment.

✺ *Boline* This is the working knife of the Witch. Often called the white-handled knife, it should have a single, sharp working edge. This is used to carve sigils onto wood, candles and so on. A blunt boline is more likely to cause accidents than a sharp one.

✺ *Other tools* There are also a few other things which can be placed on, or by, the Altar to make life easier, or for specific purposes:

A stand on which to place your Ritual outline, or any words you feel are essential to have available. The kind sold to stand cookery books on works just fine. To go with this you may need *a portable candle* so that the words can be read! In more complex Rituals you might like to appoint a 'book carrier' who can then hold the book for anyone who needs to read from it.

Matches and snuffer. The former to light candles, incense etc. The latter to extinguish them when the time comes.

Cauldron. If at any point you wish to set fire to anything, indoors or outside, then the cauldron is ideal as it contains the fire safely. Obviously, this means your cauldron must be of heatproof metal, and have sturdy legs to keep it off the ground. Equally obviously, the Cauldron does not sit on the Altar, but rather in front or under it, until it is ready to be used.

The equipment you need for your specific magical purpose. If you propose to do candle magic, you will need the candle(s), or cords for cord magic and so on. You may also need the details or a picture of the person you are working for. Initiations usually require quite a number of extras.

CREATING THE SACRED SPACE

Before you start your Ritual you will need to create your Sacred Space, or cast the Circle as it is often termed. In our Coven I tend to assign each role to a different person. If, however, you do not have enough individuals for this, then people can take more than one role. Again there are different ways of doing this but in our Coven we tend to do the following:

✦ Everyone assembles and stands in a Circle holding hands, preferably alternating male and female. We centre ourselves and recite the Witches' Rune.

✦ *The Elements on the Altar are Blessed.*

★ *The Quarters are called.* In our Coven each quarter is summoned by a different individual, whilst the rest of the group face the appropriate direction and support the caller with visualization. We commence with Air, as thought should precede action, and proceed Deosil around the Circle.

★ *The Goddess and the God are invited.* Whereas the elements are summoned, the Goddess and the God are asked if they will attend. Some groups will refer simply to the Goddess and the God, others to the Lord and Lady and yet others to specific deities by name. Most Covens have their preferred Goddess and God forms but may also choose to call upon specific deities for specific purposes.

★ *The Circle is Cast.*

There are some traditions who feel that male elements should be summoned by male Witches, others who feel that female Witches should summon male elements and vice versa. There are yet other groups who assign the roles according to level of experience. I tend not to give myself, as High Priestess, a role in creating the Sacred Space, as this leaves me free to assist any new or nervous Covenors, to magically support any part which feels less effective and even to stand in for anyone who didn't arrive as expected. It also gives me the chance to see and feel just how well each of the others is doing. It is very much up to you how you choose to assign the roles within a Ritual but I expect all my Initiates to be able to perform any, or all, of the roles in creating the Sacred Space.

RAISING ENERGY AND THE MAGICAL WORKING

I dealt with the reasons for working or not working magic, and the reasons why it might not work, in some depth in *The Real Witches' Handbook*, so here I am going to confine myself to just some of the key points:

- ⭐ *The Wiccan Rede* 'An it harm none, do what thou will.' This is the rule that Witches strive to follow, and includes harm to anyone or anything.
- ⭐ *The Law of Threefold Return* 'Whatever you do, good or ill, will be returned to you three times over.' This is not confined to magical practice, but pertains to daily life, and not just for Witches either!
- ⭐ *Be careful what you wish for* The more accurately you can phrase your wishes, the more likely you are to get what you want, otherwise you might get just what you asked for!
- ⭐ *Do not work magic to obtain money* You could inherit it from a loved one or find that it comes from an insurance claim. Instead, work for the opportunity to earn money.
- ⭐ *Be very cautious of 'love magic'* Interfering with someone's freedom of will is considered to be doing them harm. Only use magic to bring about the opportunity to meet the right person, or for increased confidence when meeting them.
- ⭐ *Temper healing with compassion and sense* Don't use healing magic to prolong suffering, nor to remove pain that is performing nature's healing function. For example, if you remove all pain from someone's broken leg, they may well use it and aggravate the injury.

In all cases you need to consider not only what is asked for, but also the potential ramifications of your actions.

Another key point to remember is that magic will often work according to need rather than desire. You may want a brand new Porsche, but receive only a second-hand banger; your need for transport has been met, even if it's not at the level you hoped for.

Magical working and raising power are entwined; there is no point in raising power unless you hold in mind the purpose, and there is no point in trying to do the working without raising the energy to make it happen. Bearing in mind that, at the planning stage, you decided what was the purpose of your Ritual, you will, of course, have the appropriate tools and equipment already on your Altar, and the purpose of the working firmly in mind. In some cases, perhaps where you are making a Talisman or an image to focus the magic through, you will have worked on these objects before creating the Sacred Space and brought them into Circle to be magically 'activated'. In other cases all of the working will take place within the Circle. In our Coven we frequently use an approach which means we raise energy to enable us to attend to the detail of the working and then we raise energy again to focus, direct and send that energy.

The most usual ways of raising energy in the Coven setting are *dance and chant*, *meditation* or *visualization*, and *Drawing Down the Moon*. There are other techniques such as astral projection, trance, binding to control the flow of blood, and scourging, but these all have associated risks and are really best handed down from Witch to Witch, rather than through a text such as this.

★ *Dancing and chanting* is by far the most common way of raising energy. Everyone in the Circle joins hands and dances Deosil around the Circle whilst a number of chants are sung. As the dance progresses it gets faster and faster until the High Priestess feels that enough energy has been built up. She then directs the release of the energy towards the focus of the magic. Dancing and chanting can be supplemented by the use of drumming, or other music. However, drumming should not be seen as an easy alternative to dancing, the drummer(s) should be able to keep time and must be able to make a contribution to the energy raised; it shouldn't be seen as a way of getting out of being seen dancing! Where space is an issue, or where you have insufficient dancers available, chanting can be used on it's own, but it is harder to raise energy this way.

There are many, many chants you can use, and you can choose whichever you like. However, the ones which are often most effective are the ones you and your Covenors write yourselves.

★ *Visualization and meditation* can encompass both raising power and the magical working in one action. Our Coven frequently works for the plight of various groups of animals, especially endangered species and their habitats. In these cases we will perform a visualization which involves the raising of power, and the focus and release of it, perhaps by raising the Earth Dragon to heal our world.

★ *Drawing Down the Moon* is a very special Rite in which the power of the Goddess is invoked into the High Priestess, by the High Priest. Some groups like to perform this at every Ritual, others save it for specific occasions. In my experience every High Priestess really looks forward to performing this Rite, until she realizes that she will need to learn the Charge of the Goddess in order to perform it well!

THE RITE OF WINE AND CAKES

This is also a way of raising power but is a separate step in the Ritual. In this case the power is raised by the High Priestess and High Priest in order to benefit the Coven itself and to further bond the unity of its members, rather than for the magical working of the Ritual. In this Rite the wine and the Chalice represent the Goddess, and the Athame represents the God. In their joining, the power of their fertility is invoked, and subsequently shared by all in the group. The cakes are symbolic of the fruitfulness of that union and also shared. This Rite, as well as bonding the group, also serves to ground (or magically earth) each of the Covenors after magical working. If you have more than 6 people in your Circle then the cakes can be started once the Chalice has been passed on from the High Priestess, but if you have fewer it is best to wait until the Chalice has been passed around the whole group before starting the cakes.

REMOVING THE CIRCLE

Once the Ritual is complete the Circle needs to be removed. All the things that have been summoned or invited should be banished or asked to return whence they came. This is very important as you do not want uninvited energies left around your home or your environment. Should you find yourself in the situation of having to abandon a Ritual part way through, you must still see to it that any invited energies are dismissed as soon as you can. It is usual to get the same person who called each quarter to dismiss it. On the rare occasion when this is not possible then it is the duty of the High Priestess to perform the banishing(s).

TIDYING UP

Having cleared everything away on the psychic plane you also need to clear up on the physical. Not only is this good practice, because it gets it over and done with, but it also means that you will get maximum help tidying away before those under pressure of time have to get away.

WRITING UP

I always encourage Covenors to write up their notes immediately after the Ritual while it is fresh in their minds. This also gives me the chance to make any notes I feel necessary, and to go around and have a quiet word with anyone who needs to speak to me. Otherwise you can find that the post-Ritual social atmosphere gets in the way. For more on this take a look at Chapter Eight, Developing the Coven.

AN EXAMPLE OF AN ESBAT RITUAL

As this is an example I have directed it at only one item of magical working. However, it is more usual to be working on several problems at an Esbat.

PURPOSE

The purpose of this Ritual is to promote healing for Anna who has a congenital defect of the hip joints. We are aware that we cannot fully cure the problem but we are working towards minimizing the arthritic changes that usually accompany the defect, towards maintaining mobility and reducing pain. We have chosen a lavender-coloured candle and magically-charged lavender oil. As Anna's Sun sign is Gemini we will inscribe her initial and the sigil for Gemini on the candle. This means that the candle, an extra candle holder, the oil and the Boline need to be on the Altar together with the usual Altar equipment.

THE RITUAL

Note: the echoing of 'Blessed Be' happens *every* time someone says it.

Everyone assembles and stands in a Circle holding hands, preferably alternating male and female.

The High Priest helps us to *centre ourselves* by guiding us through the following short meditation:

'*Take a deep breath and close your eyes. Feel the earth beneath your feet. Feel the air all around you. Feel the fire in the candles and in your hearts. Feel the water that flows though your veins. Blessed Be.*'

During the meditation everyone should be focussed on and visualizing each of the elements and their meaning.

The group echoes his 'Blessed Be'.

All together, still holding hands in a circle, we recite the *Witches' Rune*:

'*Darksome night and shining Moon, East then South, then West then North,*
Hearken to the Witches' Rune, here we come to call ye forth.
Earth and Water, Air and Fire, wand and pentacle and sword,
Work ye unto our desire, hearken ye unto our word.
Cords and censer, scourge and knife, powers of the Witches' blade,
Waken all ye unto life, come ye as the charm is laid.
Queen of Heaven, Queen of Hel, Horned Hunter of the Night,
Lend your power unto our spell, work our will by Magic Rite.
By all the power of land and sea, by all the might of Moon and Sun
As we do will so mote it be, chant the spell and be it done.'

Sometimes we will also invoke the specific Goddess(es) and God(s) by name at this point.

The High Priest then turns to the Altar to *Bless the Elements*:

He sprinkles some salt onto the Altar pentacle, describes an invoking pentagram over it with his Athame and says:

'*I do bless thee O element of Earth to make thee fit for these our Rites.*'

He kisses his forefinger, which lies along the length of the blade, then says:

'Blessed Be.'

Next, the High Priest sprinkles some incense onto the lighted charcoal, describes an invoking pentagram over it, and says:

'I do bless and consecrate thee O element of Air to make thee fit and pure for these our Rites.'

He kisses his forefinger as before, and says:

'Blessed Be.'

Then he describes an invoking pentagram in the candle flame, and says:

'I do bless and consecrate thee O element of Fire to make thee fit and pure for these our Rites.'

He kisses his forefinger as before, and says:

'Blessed Be.'

Lastly, he describes an invoking pentagram over the water, and says:

'I do bless and consecrate thee O element of Water to make thee fit and pure for these our Rites.'

He kisses his forefinger as before, and says:

'Blessed Be.'

He then stands facing the Altar, holding his hands out over the Altar, Athame in his hand, and says:

'I call on Earth to bind my spell, Air to speed its passage well, bright as Fire shall it glow and deep as ocean's tide shall flow.'

He turns to face the group, holding his Athame in both hands, blade pointing upwards, and finishes:

'Count the elements fourfold, for in the fifth the spell shall hold.'

He kisses the Athame, and says:

'Blessed Be.'

The Quarters are called. In our Coven each quarter is summoned by a different individual, whilst the rest of the group face the appropriate direction and support the caller with visualization. We commence with Air, as thought should precede action.

Standing in the East of the Circle, and facing East, the first person draws the invoking pentagram of Air and says:

'I do summon and invoke thee O element of Air. Raphael, guardian of the gateway of the East, I call upon you to be with us, to watch over us, to guard us, guide us and protect us, during these our Rites. Blessed Be.'

Standing in the South of the Circle, and facing South, the next person draws the invoking pentagram of Fire and says:

'I do summon and invoke thee O element of Fire. Michael, guardian of the gateway of the South, I call upon you to be with us, to watch over us, to guard us, guide us and protect us, during these our Rites. Blessed Be.'

Standing in the West of the Circle, and facing West the third person draws the invoking pentagram of Water and says:

'I do summon and invoke thee O element of Water. Gabriel, guardian of the gateway of the West, I call upon you to be with us, to watch over us, to guard us, guide us and protect us, during these our Rites. Blessed Be.'

Standing in the North of the Circle, and facing North, in front of the Altar if that is placed in the North, the fourth person draws the invoking pentagram of Earth and says:

'I do summon and invoke thee O element of Earth. Uriel, guardian of the gateway of the North, I call upon you to be with us, to watch over us, to guard us, guide us and protect us, during these our Rites. Blessed Be.'

The *Goddess and the God* are invited. A Witch steps forwards and stands, facing North, before the Altar, arms upraised, and visualizes the Goddess and the God. When they are fixed firmly in the Witch's mind, the Witch says:

'I call upon the Old Gods, upon Hecate and Herne, Ceridwyn and Cernunnos, to be with us this night. I ask them to watch over us to guard us, guide us and protect us, during these our Rites. Blessed Be.'

The *Circle is Cast*. One person takes either an Athame or the Sword and, starting from the North East corner of the Circle and moving Deosil, will describe a Circle around the outside of the working space, saying:

'I do conjure this Circle as a place of power and protection, a place between the worlds, and a time out of time. Blessed Be.'

The Circle is drawn until it overlaps at the North Eastern point again. As this is happening, everyone visualizes an electric blue circle being drawn around the group. This circle spreads and becomes an all-encompassing sphere of light. Tall Witches can usually do this by raising their Athame or Sword over the heads of the surrounding circle of Witches. Shorter Witches need the Circle of Witches to move towards the centre of the Circle so that the Circle caster can walk around them. This helps to prevent a wave of ducking Witches!

POWER RAISING AND THE MAGICAL WORKING

Power is raised through *dance and chant*:

Two drummers stand aside and everyone else joins hands and dances Deosil. All chant. We start off gently and increase both the speed and volume so that we work towards a peak. We usually do 3 or 4 chants with 3 or 4 repetitions of each, for example:

'Isis, Astarte, Diana, Hecate, Demeter, Kali, Innana' (repeat 3 more times).

'Lady of the Moon, Lady of the Moon, Come to us, be with us, Lady of the Moon' (repeat 2 more times).

'We all come from the Goddess, and to her we shall return, like a drop of rain flowing to the ocean.' (This one is slightly more complex as on the first, second and third repetitions the women repeat the above verse, whilst the men chant competitively:)

'We all come from the Horned God, and to him we shall return, like an autumn leaf floating to the forest floor.'

Sometimes, in order to ring the changes I will reverse the male and female roles in this!

We finish with:

'Isis, Astarte, Diana, Hecate, Demeter, Kali, Innana' (repeat 3 more times).

The High Priestess then takes the healing candle and carves the initial A and the sigil for Gemini. She then passes it through the incense smoke and says:

'I call on Air to bring healing to Anna.'

She passes it quickly through the flame of the Altar candle and says:

'I call upon Fire to bring healing to Anna.'

She sprinkles it with a little water and says:

'I call upon Water to bring healing to Anna.'

She sprinkles it with salt and says:

'I call upon Earth to bring healing to Anna.'

She then anoints the candle with the oil, placing a couple of drops on the centre of the candle and massaging it towards the ends. Whilst she does so she visualizes Anna and the healing processes we are seeking. When she feels she has charged the candle with healing energy, she says:

'Blessed Be.'

She then passes the candle to the person on her left, who repeats the massaging process. The candle passes all around the Circle, with everyone adding their own energy, but not more oil, until it reaches the High Priestess again. She then holds the candle over the Altar pentacle and says:

'I call upon the Old Gods, upon Hecate and Herne, Ceridwyn and Cernunnos, to send their healing powers to Anna, to watch over her and protect her. Blessed Be.'

She then places the candle in the candle holder and lights it from the Altar candle. The candle in its holder is placed on the Altar pentagram.

The dancers then join hands and repeat the dancing and chanting from earlier. The High Priestess must focus on Anna and on the energy raised, and at the culmination of the chanting and dancing she brings her arms up, thus causing all the other dancers to raise theirs. At this point she releases the power, mentally directing it at Anna. Everyone else should be focussing in the same way, but it is the High Priestess's responsibility to actually direct the combined energies. Once she is happy that the energy has been sent to its destination, she lowers her arms, bringing everyone else's arms down at the same time. There is a short pause while everyone gets their breath and balance back and then the hands are released. Everyone then returns to their places in the Circle with the High Priestess and High Priest standing in front of the Altar.

THE RITE OF WINE AND CAKES

The High Priest then takes the Chalice of wine and holds it up in front of the group, and says:

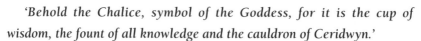

'*Behold the Chalice, symbol of the Goddess, for it is the cup of wisdom, the fount of all knowledge and the cauldron of Ceridwyn.*'

He then turns to face the High Priestess and kneels facing her.

The High Priestess then takes her Athame and holds it in both hands, point upwards, so that the whole group can see it, and says:

'*Behold the Athame, symbol of the Horned God.*'

She turns to face the High Priest and, looking him in the eyes, lowers the Athame, point first, into the wine, and says:

'*As the Cup is to the female, so the Athame is to the male.*'

The High Priest and High Priestess then continue together:

'*And co-joined together they bring forth life eternal.*'

They pause and then say together:

'*Blessed Be.*'

The High Priestess removes the Athame from the wine and replaces it in her belt, or on the Altar. The High Priest rises and then holds the Chalice in both hands, out towards the High Priestess. She also holds it with both her hands. He kisses her on each cheek, saying:

'*In perfect love and perfect trust. Blessed Be.*'

She repeats his '*Blessed Be*' (note: on this occasion the rest of the group will not echo the Blessed Be), then kisses him on each cheek, saying:

'*In perfect love and perfect trust. Blessed Be.*'

He repeats her Blessed Be, and releases the Chalice. She takes a sip of the wine and then turns to the person on her left and repeats the process. The Chalice passes around the Circle until it is handed back to the High Priest who, after his sip, replaces it on the Altar.

The High Priest then takes the plate of cakes and again kneels before the High Priestess. She draws an invoking pentagram over the cakes and says:

'I do bless and consecrate these cakes, symbol of the fruitfulness and bounty of the Great Mother. Blessed Be.'

The High Priest then rises to his feet and offers the High Priestess the cakes in the same way as he did the wine. The cakes thus also pass around the Circle with everyone taking one, and eating it. (Note: it is important that each person passes the cakes onto their neighbour before tasting their own. Otherwise, they tend to pebbledash their neighbour with partly-eaten biscuit!)

Once everyone has finished chewing, the High Priest says:

'Let those who summoned the elements, now bid them depart.'

The person who invoked Air now stands in the East, facing East and, drawing the banishing pentagram of Air, says:

'I do banish thee O element of Air. Raphael, guardian of the gateway to the East I give you thanks for your presence, for watching over us, guarding, guiding and protecting us and I bid you hale and farewell. Blessed Be.'

This is then repeated, for each of the elements, at each of the quarters.

The person who invited the Goddess and the God steps forward and stands before the Altar, facing North and, holding their hands up, says:

'I give thanks to the Old Gods, to Hecate and Herne, Ceridwyn and Cernunnos, for being with us this night, for watching over us, guarding, guiding and protecting us. Hale and farewell. Blessed Be.'

The person who cast the Circle now takes the Sword or their Athame and, once again starting at the North East and proceeding Deosil, says:

'I remove this Circle and return this space to its own time and its own place. Blessed Be.'

Everyone joins hands and the High Priestess says:

'Our Circle is ended, but our fellowship is unbroken and so we say: (at this point everyone joins in to say together:) *Merry Meet, Merry Part and Merry Meet Again. Blessed Be.'*

This is a very simple example of an Esbat Ritual, and you may choose to elaborate it if you feel that you and your Coven are able and willing to do more. Having said that, it can be better to start off with a few straightforward Rituals until the group has established itself and at least a couple of the Covenors have confidence in what they are doing. After that time everyone will find it less stressful to gradually take on more magical work until you feel that the Coven has reached a sensible limit of what it can achieve at an Esbat. If you are too ambitious to begin with, you will find yourself putting so much personal energy into the working that you are quite worn out for some time afterwards.

SEVEN

SABBAT CELEBRATIONS

The eight Sabbats which go to make up the Wheel of the Year are times of great celebration for Witches. Whenever possible Witches will gather together; Covens, daughter Covens, perhaps some Solitaries who are well known to the High Priestess, and sometimes Aspirants invited to attend the Ritual and its subsequent feast. Some groups will also devise celebrations which the whole family can join in (some ideas on this can be found in *The Real Witches' Kitchen*). The Sabbats mark the passage of the seasons and bring us closer to the natural cycles of the land. They are also times when we re-enact the stories of the Goddess and the God, which brings us closer understanding and appreciation of the Divine.

The eight Sabbats are divided into two groups; the major and the minor Sabbats. The minor Sabbats are those which link to the cycle of the Sun; the Summer and Winter Solstices and the Spring and Autumn Equinoxes. The dates of these Solar events vary slightly from year to year, due to the Earth not taking precisely 365 days to orbit the Sun. Some Covens will choose to hold their Rituals on the actual date, some on the usual date, and others will choose a date close to the event which suits as many Covenors as possible. The major Sabbats are Samhain, Imbolg, Beltane and Lammas. Again, some Covens will hold their Ritual on the usual date, whereas others will select the date which enables most people to attend. Another approach is to look to natural indicators to time your festival, eg holding Beltane when the Hawthorn (or May) blossoms. Every festival is considered to have a three day 'window'; the day before, or eve of the Sabbat, the date of the Sabbat, or the day after. None of these is right or wrong; as our forebears did not have access to an accurate calendar they would not have been able to use precise dating. Many Covens will hold 'closed' (Initiates or Covenors only) Rituals for the major Sabbats and 'open' Rituals for the minor, where the atmosphere is deliberately lighter.

There are many ways of devising Rituals for the Sabbats. Some Covens have set Rituals which they carry out without variation from year to year. Others prefer to customize their Rituals according to the needs of the group, the number of people attending, or just so that they can experience different aspects of the festival. In this chapter I intend to give an introduction to each Sabbat and some ideas as to how you might wish to put these into Ritual form. These are not meant to be definitive Rituals, simply suggestions that you can take and make your own, by adding or subtracting material as you wish. Remember, there is no 'one right way' to honour the Goddess and the God; in the Craft it is for each of us to find the way which is most meaningful to us. In my group I try to ensure that each Ritual is meaningful to everyone present by giving each some part to play. In order to expand our knowledge and experience I also like to get Initiates to research and write new Rites and Rituals for the group. However, if you are doing this it is a good idea to ensure that you go over the Ritual with the writer to check that it is both sensible and suitable for the group. Things to bear in mind include:

☆ *Purpose* The purpose of a Sabbat Ritual is to celebrate that point in the Wheel of the Year as a part of the Wheel, not in isolation. It is also to gain a deeper

understanding of the Sabbat, the Wheel, the Goddess and the God, and the way these all mesh together. The more each person puts into a Sabbat Ritual the more they will actually experience of the Divine, and the deeper will be their understanding and personal contact.

★ *Relevance* Occasionally people can get so carried away by their own preferences or current realm of study that they produce a Ritual which, whilst interesting, is not actually relevant to either the Craft or the Coven. I remember one hugely amusing Ritual constructed around the Quabbala, but regrettably none of the rest of the Coven had much experience or interest in this Hebraic system and so found themselves trying to perform Rites which they didn't really understand, and read words they couldn't pronounce. It is important that the Ritual also has some relevance to daily life, so that everyone can actually gain something from the experience.

★ *Practicality* However wonderful the idea, there is little point trying to hold Rites which do not fit your location, which require everyone to be super-fit, or which require skills your Covenors do not have. Similarly, you need to ensure that any tools, equipment, herbs, flowers, etc, are actually available.

★ *Completeness* This sounds obvious, but it is always as well to ensure that your Ritual has a beginning a middle and an end. Not only that but it should actually reflect the Sabbat in question.

★ *Length* Whilst we want to do honour to the Goddess and the God and make the Ritual meaningful, an over-long Ritual is just as bad as one that is too short. In the case of the former, it is not possible to maintain high levels of concentration for hours on end. Not to mention that some people will need to go home and get some sleep afterwards. I have attended a Ritual where we were still creating the Sacred Space after two hours! Over-short Rituals can leave everyone feeling flat, if not actually cheated.

BASIC OUTLINE OF A SABBAT RITUAL

Whilst mostly similar to any other Ritual, the Sabbat Ritual differs in some key aspects. In outline it is as follows:

★ *The location is prepared.* Whether the Ritual is to take place indoors or outside, the same preparations need to be made as for an Esbat, see Chapter Six, page 101.

★ *Everyone arrives and prepares themselves.* A key part of personal preparation will be to ensure that everyone knows what they are going to be doing and where it fits into the overall Ritual. If you have written your Ritual well in advance it should be possible to give advance notice of roles, so long as you know everyone will turn up. Otherwise you will need to allow a little time at the start of the Ritual for studying the outline and any individual roles. If your Covenors have been with you for a while they will probably be pretty much aware of the requirements of different parts. If they are newer you may need to give some guidance as to what you expect them to say, do and visualize.

★ *The group assembles for the Ritual Explanation.* As in the Esbat the group forms a circle, preferably alternating male and female. At this point it is a good idea to explain the Ritual, ie to run through what is going to happen and who will be doing what. This needs to be done by the person who actually wrote the Ritual and assigned the roles, so that they can clear up any misunderstandings.

★ *The Witches' Rune.* In my Coven the High Priest leads us in a very short meditation and then we all chant the Witches' Rune, which is given in Chapter Six, on page 116.

⭐ *The Sacred Space is created.* The Elements are Blessed, the Quarters called, and the Goddess and the God invited in the same way as for an Esbat. You may prefer to invoke the Goddess and the God by names which reflect the point of the Wheel of the Year. Note that, unless you are working magic, it is not necessary to actually cast the Circle, as you will not be raising power.

⭐ *The Sabbat Introduction is given.* This is not the same as the Ritual Explanation, as the Sabbat Introduction should talk about the festival and its meanings rather than the more practical detail of who does what. I like to assign this role to one of the group members, who will write it in their own words. Those with experience can often be relied upon to do it on the spur of the moment, but it is kinder to give newer Covenors a bit of warning so that they have time to prepare.

⭐ *The essence of the Ritual takes place.* This is the centre-piece of the Ritual, the purpose. Here you may enact one of the stories of the Goddess and God, or perform some Rite which reflects upon the agricultural cycle, or the meaning of the Sabbat. There is more on this later. It is worth noting that it is not sufficient for everyone to just go through the motions of Ritual. Whilst the Ritual is happening everyone should be focussing on the inner meaning of the Rites they are enacting or observing. For example, at Imbolg the wishes each person says are a series of spells asking the Goddess and the God for the things we want for the coming season; the lighting of the candles symbolizes the return of Spring; the chants are urging the return of the Goddess as Maiden, and the unveiling of the High Priestess is symbolic of this actually occurring.

⭐ *The Rite of Wine and Cakes is performed.* This is performed in the same way as for an Esbat, although where you have given the roles of the Goddess and the God to Covenors it can be empowering for them to perform this Rite together. Alternatively, you might like to have the Witches who perform the Rite go around to every Covenor and give them the Chalice, male to female and female to male, rather than it passing around the Circle.

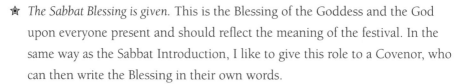

★ *The Sabbat Blessing is given.* This is the Blessing of the Goddess and the God upon everyone present and should reflect the meaning of the festival. In the same way as the Sabbat Introduction, I like to give this role to a Covenor, who can then write the Blessing in their own words.

★ *The Sacred Space is removed.* Once more this is performed in the same way as for an Esbat. Some Covens like to hold the Sabbat feast within the Sacred Space, but this means leaving the Goddess and the God, as well as the Elements, effectively hanging around whilst everyone parties. Not to mention that, unless you have lots of space to arrange food close to the Circle, the moving backwards and forwards to bring foods to the Circle seems somewhat contrary to the spirit of what has passed before. Also, if the feasting waits until the Circle has been removed then everyone can relax and enjoy themselves, and the High Priestess does not have to worry that people will 'feast' so well that they cannot banish the Quarters, or perform other actions!

★ *The Feast takes place.* Of course you can purchase and prepare all the food and drink yourself. However, it is far more reasonable to ask everyone to bring a contribution. Don't, however, just leave it at that, I have seen a feast where everyone brought bread and cheese, which, whilst perfectly edible, can be somewhat tedious! So it's a good idea to have some kind of consensus as to who will bring what. I find that discussing this at the end of the previous Ritual is probably the easiest way, as everyone can hear what the others intend to contribute. Ideally, Sabbat feasts should be of seasonal food and drink, and, where possible of produce local to your area.

SAMHAIN

Samhain, All Hallows Eve, All Souls, Halloween, takes place on October 31 and is the most important festival in the Witches' calendar. It is both the beginning and end of the Witches' year, in a similar way to New Year's Eve. It is the time when the Goddess takes on her robes of Crone and the God rides out on the Wild Hunt to collect the souls of the dead. In times past it would be the time when the harvest was ended, or nearly so, and thus it marks the start of the resting season for the land. It is a time when the veil between the worlds of life and death is at its thinnest, a time for remembering the dead, and a time for scrying.

A SAMHAIN RITUAL

For this Ritual you will be creating a Dark Circle and a Light Circle, so you will need two areas or two rooms. This Ritual centres around using the time between the worlds to scry into the unknown. In the Ritual the High Priestess presides over this world to assist the rest of the Coven to see what might be learned. As it can explore parts of the personality which are untried it is not really a suitable Ritual for non-Initiates. If you do feel that you would like non-Initiates to attend then you might like to consider not allowing them to enter the Dark Circle.

One area or room should be almost completely dark, lit only by a single night-light in a dark glass. If possible it should also be quite chilly and unadorned. In the centre of the area you need a bowl of water to which some black paint or ink has been added to create a Dark Mirror. If it is possible, arrange this so that the light of the Moon is reflected in the water. If you are indoors you might also burn some incense with earthy woody tones such as musk, sandalwood, myrrh and frankincense. This room or area is representing the underworld so, as High Priestess, you can make it as other-worldly as you feel appropriate, but please try to stop short of overdoing the plastic Halloween decorations – it's not a kiddies party! Try not to let the Covenors see the Dark Circle until it is their turn to visit it, or to tell them what awaits them there.

The second area or room should have the Altar and plenty of light. This is the Light Circle and it is here that everyone gathers.

After the Sabbat Introduction, the High Priest stands in the centre of the Circle facing the High Priestess who stands before the Altar. She stands upright with her arms folded across her chest, hands resting on opposite shoulders. He raises his arms and says:

'Now is the start of the dark part of the year. Winter and the time of resting and reflection are upon us. Now is the time for the Goddess to

take on the robes of the Crone. I call upon the Wise Mother to attend and be with this our High Priestess, to lend her wisdom and guidance.'

He draws an invoking pentagram over the High Priestess. If the High Priestess has a hooded robe, she should raise the hood, or she might like to put on a cloak. Note that the High Priest is *not* invoking the Crone into the High Priestess, but asking that she should be guided by the wisdom of the Goddess as Crone. The High Priestess then leaves the Light Circle and goes to the Dark Circle. Here she ensures that all is ready, the incense is burning, the Dark Mirror reflects a little light from the one candle and adds any last-minute touches to the decor to increase the atmosphere. She then settles herself down in the North, behind the Dark Mirror. It is worth noting that you need to make yourself comfortable, especially if there are a lot of people in your group, as you could be here some time. In the Light Circle the High Priest turns and says to the others:

'This is the Circle of light and of life, our High Priestess has gone from us to the world of the Crone, to seek knowledge, wisdom and understanding. Who here is willing to follow in her steps and learn what might be known?'

He then directs the first person to visit the Crone. They leave the Light Circle and proceed to the Dark Circle where they should ask permission to enter. The High Priestess will then ask them to come and kneel at the other side of the Dark Mirror and say:

'Behold the waters of life and death. Here you might see all manner of things; from your deepest secrets to things that may yet happen. If you are certain you wish to know then you may seek knowledge now.'

She stirs the waters with a stick or wand, and indicates that the Covenor should look. It is up to you whether you wish to allow them as much time as they wish, or whether you wish to indicate that they

have had long enough by once again stirring the water and bidding them return to the Light Circle. The Covenor then returns to the Light Circle, where they do not talk about what they have experienced. The High Priest then sends the next person to the Dark Circle, where the process is repeated.

If your group is small, those waiting in the Light Circle can chant whilst each person is away. However, if you have more than, say, 6 members they might find this tiring after a while. In my Coven we pass the time by telling tales and stories suitable to the season, including ghost stories.

The last person to visit the Dark Circle is the High Priest. After he has scryed he returns to the Light Circle and winds up whatever activity is occurring there and everyone should chant gently while they await the High Priestess's return. After the departure of the High Priest from the Dark Circle, the High Priestess may like to take her turn at scrying, before removing any decorations she does not want seen in full light.

The High Priestess then returns to the Light Circle where the Rite of Wine and Cakes takes place.

Here are some other ideas:

★ *Remembering those who have gone before.* This is a good time to reflect on the lives of those who have died. I am not talking about mourning the dead, but rather about remembering them in terms of the good times we shared and the gifts of good memories they left us. Some groups also like to remember those who suffered and died during the Witch Hunts.

★ *The Wild Hunt.* If you have access to some fairly unused woodland you can enact the Wild Hunt. Get a sensible member of the Coven to check out and

set a course through the woods, which must be completed by each individual without stopping, looking back or deviating from the assigned path.

YULE

The Winter Solstice takes place on or around 21 December, according to the Earth's movement around the Sun. A good quality diary or almanac will give you the exact date each year. The Winter Solstice marks the end of the days of decreasing light, and the start of the days of increasing light. It is the shortest day of the year. Here we remember that even in the depths of winter, there is a promise of the return of spring and summer, of light and warmth. The Goddess and the God are still in their dark aspects but we celebrate the rebirth of the Sun, and the return of the Oak King, Lord of the lengthening days.

A YULE RITUAL

In advance of this Ritual you will need to prepare a Yule Log, or get someone in the Coven to do it for you. Find a log which rests firmly on a flat surface; you may need to get someone to saw off the lower surface to ensure this. Then either drill a number of holes, large enough to each take a small candle, in the top, or hammer in a number of nails in a pattern which allows candles to be wedged between them. The log will need to be large enough to accommodate sufficient candles for everyone attending the Ritual to have one. If you have space the log is best placed on its own small table, or stand, in the centre of the Circle, otherwise place it at the centre front of the Altar.

Each member of the group will need to prepare a few words to welcome and encourage the return of the Sun, and to speak of their hopes for the coming season.

After the Sabbat Explanation everyone joins hands and walks Deosil around the Circle, chanting verses to honour the season. When the chants are finished the High Priestess stands before the Altar facing the group, and says:

'Here in the darkest part of the year we are in the midst of winter, but even in the depths of darkness there is the promise of light to come. At Yule the spark of light is born, and from that spark the Sun will grow in strength and beauty through the seasons. Blessed Be.'

She then lights a taper from the Altar candle and holds it up before the rest of the group, before lighting the first candle on the Yule Log and speaking of her hopes. When she has finished, she passes the candle on to the person on her left who then lights a candle and speaks of their hopes. This goes on all around the Circle until everyone has had their turn. (Note: when lighting a series of candles it is

best to start at the back of the cluster, so that following Covenors do not have to try to reach over the flames to light their candles.)

When everyone has finished the High Priestess turns to the group and says:

'*Behold the candles burn brightly, just as the Sun will burn brighter and brighter in the coming days. May the Sun God bring life and vitality to the land. May the Goddess and the God bring fertility and prosperity to the land and to each and every one of us. Blessed Be.*'

If you wish you can have more chanting and dancing here, but make sure that the dancers do not either extinguish the flames, or set fire to their hair or robes as they pass! The Rite of Wine and Cakes is then performed.

Some other ideas:

★ *Rise to greet the reborn Sun.* Some groups will rise before dawn and go out to a high point where they can wait to see the Sun rise. Before Sunrise they will sing, dance and drum to 'call the Sun up'. During Sunrise they will express hopes and wishes for the Season. Afterwards there will be more chanting and drumming to welcome the newly reborn Sun. This is not as arduous as it at first appears as Sunrise at Yule, in the UK at least, does not take place until around 8am. However, it is worth mentioning that you need to find a fairly isolated spot, as your neighbours may not take kindly to the noise at that time of day! It is also worth taking the time to practise the drumming. I know I'm not the only person to wonder if an unpractised, out of time cacophony produced by out of tune drums isn't more likely to frighten the Sun, not to mention the wildlife, away.

★ *Enacting the battle of the Oak and Holly Kings.* The part of the year where the days decrease in length (from Litha to Yule) is presided over by the Holly

King. The other half is presided over by the Oak King. These two brothers, who are but different aspects of the whole, fight at Yule and at Litha for dominion over the forthcoming half-year. Some Covens enact this fight, having two combatants taking the roles of Holly and Oak King. If you plan to do this, it is a good idea to ensure that the two 'Kings' rehearse well, not only so that the 'right' King wins, but also so that they do not do any real injury to one another.

IMBOLG

Imbolg, also known as Oimelc, the feast of Bride and Candlemass, takes place around 2 February and is the first of spring. The first buds are seen on the trees, the first flowers strike up through the frozen ground. Imbolg literally means 'in the belly' and at this time the first sheep are in lamb. The Goddess changes her robes of Crone for those of the Maiden.

AN IMBOLG RITUAL

In advance of the Ritual everyone will need to find, or write, and then commit to memory, a piece of verse, prose, music, or song which reflects the spirit of the season. This should include some expression of the changes in nature and of wanted changes in that person's life. It is important that the pieces are memorized as there will not be enough light to read from bits of paper until well into the Ritual. The High Priestess' piece should include her hopes for the Coven as a whole as well as any personal wishes. Have one candle for each person spaced around the outside edge of the Circle, and two on the Altar. If you are working outdoors the candles will have to be in jars so that, when lit, any wind does not blow them out. The Ritual commences in darkness with only one candle lit on the Altar, the rest of the room or space remaining in darkness. The High Priestess should have a dark veil over her head, and wear a dark cloak over her robes. If you can, wear white robes or a long white dress under the dark cloak.

After the Sabbat Introduction the group chants:

'Return, return, by earth and air, by fire and by water,' three times.

The person to the left of the High Priestess recites his or her piece for the festival. Then the High Priestess lights a taper from the Altar candle and passes it to the person to her left, who lights the candle behind him or her. The group chants again and the process is repeated all around the Circle, until all the surrounding candles are lit. The last person to give their piece is the High Priest. The High Priestess does not give her recitation yet. Having given his piece and lit his candle, the High Priest steps forward into the centre of the Circle and says:

'The season of lights is upon us. We say farewell to the winter, to the time of resting, and look forward to the Spring which brings us fresh starts and new beginnings. I call upon the Old Ones (gives names of the

Coven's preferred Deities) *to return to us the Maiden, the Goddess of youthful energy and fresh growth.'*

He turns around to face the High Priestess in front of the Altar and, drawing the pentagram over her body, says:

'By seed and root, by stem and bud, by leaf and flower and fruit do we invoke thee, fair Lady of the Spring.'

Two of the other Covenors then step forward and remove the High Priestess's dark cloak and veil. The High Priest then gives the High Priestess the Fivefold Blessing (you will find this in the First Degree Initiation Ritual, page 72) and welcomes the Goddess as Maiden. She then delivers her piece to the whole group and lights her candle, which should be the second of the two Altar candles. At this point you might like to have other chants, and perhaps some circle dancing, before moving on to the Rite of Wine and Cakes.

Some other ideas:

★ *Crown of Lights.* As an alternative to the ring of lights surrounding the group, some like to make a crown of lights for the High Priestess to wear as a symbol of the returning Maiden aspect. Those who are technically minded may be able to create something which runs off a battery pack concealed about the High Priestess's person, but the rest of us will need to construct the crown using candles. As you can imagine this needs great care and attention as it is important that the candles are secure, do not set light to, or drip wax onto, the High Priestess' hair!

★ *The festival of Bride.* Here the Ritual is dedicated to the Goddess Bride (pronounced Breed) or Brigid as she is also known. The women in the group prepare an image of the Goddess from straw and dress her all in white. They also prepare a bed. The men in the group prepare a phallic wand or club.

During the Ritual the women place Bride in her bed, and the men place the wand alongside her. This symbolizes the union of the Goddess and the God for the fertility of all. In times past the images in their bed would be placed by or in the fire so that they might burn away overnight. Today, it is somewhat safer and more practical to do one of the following. Place the bed on one side, burning a candle at each end for a supervised period for three days, before dismantling it. Or take it outside of the house before burning it carefully.

OESTARA

Oestara, or Oestre, marks the Spring Equinox on or around 21 March, a time when day and night are equal, a time of balance. From now on the length of daylight exceeds the length of darkness. As with the Solstices and the Autumn Equinox you will need an almanac or good calendar to work out exactly which day this falls on in any year. This is the festival of the European Spring Goddess Eostre or Eostar, who derives from both Ishtar and Astarte. Her symbols are the egg of birth and rebirth, and the hare. It is the time when Persephone returns from the underworld to bring new life to the land. It is also the festival of the dying and rising Gods such as Attis, Mithras, Tammuz, Adonis and Osiris. Here we see the signs that Spring is well and truly with us, and, in keeping with the theme of balance, it is a time for turning out the old and taking on the new.

AN OESTARA RITUAL

In this Ritual we will be emphasizing that theme of balance. If you can, find two cauldrons, or other fireproof vessels, and place one or two nightlights in the bottom of each. You will also need a number of small pieces of paper and some pencils. In the preparation time just before Ritual get each person to write on one piece of paper the things they wish to get rid of and on another the things they wish to begin. These can be practical things such as giving up smoking and starting a course of study, they can be emotional thoughts and feelings, or things directly related to the Craft. The Covenors should bring these papers into Circle with them, taking care not to get them mixed up!

> **After the Sabbat Explanation the High Priestess stands before the Altar and addresses the group:**
> *'Dark gives way to light, the days increase in length. Now is the time for us to move from darkness into light, to cast off that which is no longer needful.'*
> **She lights a taper from the Altar candle and lights the candles in the first Cauldron, saying:**
> *'This is the fire of the old, let it burn away the things we no longer need. Blessed Be.'*

Then each person in turn places their paper with the things they wish to get rid of into the flames, perhaps stating out loud their wishes or simply saying:

'Goddess Eostar take from me these things which I no longer need. Blessed Be.'

(Note: if performing this indoors you may wish to consider the potential effects on any smoke alarm you may have fitted.) Next, the High Priest steps forward and addresses the group:

'Dark gives way to light, the days increase in length. Now is the time for us to move from darkness into light, to take on new hopes and aspirations.'

He lights the taper from the first Cauldron and lights the candle(s) in the second one, saying:

'This is the fire of the new, let it bring to us those things which are needful for us to grow in the light of the Old Gods. Blessed Be.'

Into these flames are placed the papers stating the things people wish to take on. These segments of Ritual can be separated by chanting and/or dancing if you wish. The Rite of Wine and Cakes is then performed.

Some other ideas:

✩ *The Dying and Rising God.* In this Ritual the High Priest plays the role of the God who dies; the High Priestess plays the part of the Goddess who gives him life again. Choose, from any of a number of the tales of the Goddess and the God, a story which you feel is appropriate to your group, and their abilities. Try to find enough roles for everyone to have some part, however small. As High Priestess and High Priest are playing the parts of the Goddess and the God, you might like to change the Rite of Wine and Cakes so that the High Priestess offers the wine to each of the men in Circle, and the High Priest does likewise to the women.

✦ *Runic Eggs.* On its own this does not really constitute a central theme to the Sabbat, but can be added to the Ritual or take place during the feasting. As Eostar is a Northern European Goddess, use of the Runes is quite appropriate in her festival. Prior to the Ritual, hard boil a number of eggs, one for each Covenor plus an extra one. Decorate each with a different Runic symbol. Try to select symbols which are rich in meaning, and place them in a bowl covered with a cloth on the Altar. At the designated point each person slips their hand under the cloth and selects at random an egg. The fun is then in interpreting the Runes in a way appropriate to each individual!

BELTANE

Also known as Bealtaine, Walpurgisnacht, May Day, Beltane falls on 1 May. This is the second most important festival in the Wheel of the Year. This is also a day

when the veil between the worlds is thin, but rather than a time when the dead are remembered it is a day when the trickster Gods are to the fore, eg Pan, Puck and Loki. For this reason it is not a good time for divination as readings may have convoluted or unexpected meanings. It is the time when the Goddess discards her robes of Maiden and takes on those of Mother. The youthful God returns to her side and we celebrate the marriage of the Goddess and the God. The traditions of the Queen of the May and the Maypole reflect this wedding.

A BELTANE RITUAL

In advance of the Ritual you will need to make a cloak or coat, and a crown suitable for a Jester, together with his staff of office. The staff usually has bells, balloons and streamers attached to it. You will also need crowns, and perhaps cloaks too, for a May Queen and May King. You might also like to prepare a list of tasks, riddles, forfeits, and so on for the participants to do during the central part of the Ritual. These might include reciting poetry, singing a song, kissing everyone on the nose, and so on. Be as imaginative as you can, and try to ensure that at least some of the tasks have direct relevance to the Craft.

Once the whole group has arrived, write everyone's names, except yours as your role remains that of High Priestess, onto slips of paper and place them into a bag or hat. The first female name out of the bag is to be the May Queen, the first male will be the Jester. The May Queen chooses her own May King, so his name is not selected at random. Two other Covenors should be selected to be the lords and/or ladies in waiting. Place two chairs, as thrones, on either side of the Altar, or if space permits together in front of the Altar. Leave space between the chairs for the Jester to stand.

After the Sabbat Explanation everyone should join hands and dance around the Circle, with the High Priestess in the centre. They can chant as they go if you wish. Once the chanting and dancing have finished the High Priestess will stand between the chairs in front of the Altar and call forward the female chosen to be May Queen. The High Priestess says:

'Now is the time when the Goddess sheds her robes of Maiden and takes on those of the Mother, and the God descends to be by her side. For joined together they bring forth life, fruitfulness and fertility to all. Blessed Be.'

Once the group have echoed her *'Blessed Be'*, she continues:

'Tonight, in celebration of the marriage of the Goddess and the God, we call forth (name of the chosen May Queen) to be our May Queen.'

The May Queen steps forward. The High Priestess continues:

'We robe her and crown her and do her honour.'

The lords and/or ladies in waiting place the robe around her shoulders and the crown on her head, and lead her to her throne, where she sits. Then each person in the Circle steps forward (taking care to walk Deosil around the Circle), and bows before her saying:

'Hail to the Queen of the May.'

If you wish they may kiss her on the hand, or on each cheek. The May Queen then stands and says:

'As Queen of the May it is my right and my privilege to select the King who will sit beside me. And so I call (the name of her chosen May King) to step forward and take his place by my side.'

The chosen May King steps forward. The lords and/or ladies in waiting hand the robe and crown to the May Queen, who crowns and robes her King and then leads him to his throne. Before he sits he turns to the Queen and says:

'Gracious Lady I give thanks to thee for this honour. I am glad that we shall rule this night together.'

He kisses her and they both take their seats. Then each person in the Circle steps forward (taking care to walk Deosil around the Circle), and bows before the King saying:

'Hail to the King of the May.'

The King then rises and says:

'This is the night of Beltane, the feast of the marriage of the Goddess and the God so it is fit that we have someone to take charge of our celebrations. I call upon (name of the Jester) to step forward.'

The King sits and the Jester steps forward and kneels before the King and Queen. The Queen says:

'Bring forth his cap and bells, that all may know him for our Jester.'

The lords and/or ladies in waiting bring the Jester's cloak and crown and dress him. They give the staff to the Queen, who hands it to the Jester. The Jester then rises and says:

'I thank thee my King and Queen for this honour. For it is known that the Jester is the Fool, and the Fool is the first, for we are each the Fool when we start out. Hence all must obey his wishes.'

The Jester then dances around the Circle generally playing up to his title. He may tickle Covenors, or strike them with the balloons, etc. Once he has completed the circuit he returns and stands between the King and Queen. He then takes the list of tasks and selects who does what. No-one should be exempt from the games, not the King and Queen, or the High Priestess and High Priest.

This is not meant to be a solemn Ritual, but should be full of humour and laughter. Not only is it the celebration of the marriage of the Goddess and the God, but it is also a reminder to us that,

whatever our rank or status, we are all equal in the Craft, and subject to the will of the Gods.

Once everyone has completed one or two tasks the Jester calls a halt:

'The day draws on and the games are over. Now we turn to our King and Queen and ask their Blessings upon us.'

The Jester then takes his place to the left of the Queen, and the King and Queen celebrate the Rite of Wine and Cakes, supported by the High Priestess and High Priest.

We like to continue the theme into the feasting, with the Queen and King being waited upon and the Jester continuing to set tasks for the other Covenors. This includes the tasks of clearing away!

Some other ideas:

⭐ *Handfasting.* This is not a theme as such, but we find that rarely a year goes past without someone wishing to be Handfasted at Beltane. Handfasting is the Witches' wedding and so Beltane is a very significant date to choose for this. The main differences between a Handfasting and the more orthodox weddings are that in the Handfasting the couple come together to the Circle as equals, no-one 'gives the Bride away'. They write and make their own unique vows to each other. They also continue the traditions of the tying of hands (hence Handfasting), and of jumping the broom (to signify the leap from the single life to a joint one).

⭐ *The Bel Fire.* Named after the Fire God Bel. It used to be traditional in rural areas for two fires to be lit, and for all livestock to be driven between them, both for purification and for fertility. Young people would jump the fires, older ones would again pass between them. This can be enacted by having two candles, or small fires if you can contain them safely, and for everyone to pass between them. Note that it is not wise for people to jump the flames if they are wearing robes or other loose clothing. Fertility is not just about reproduction, it is also creativity, new ideas, work, studies, relationships and all other areas of our lives. So we can also create symbols of the things we wish fertility for in the coming season, and pass these over or between the Bel fires. For example, for me this could be the representation of a book!

LITHA

Litha, The Summer Solstice, falls in the middle of summer, around 21 June. Midsummer is the longest day. It is the point at which the length of daylight starts to shorten again. It is a time of paradox in that, even as the Sun reaches the height of its power, it begins to wane. Like the other Solstice and the Equinoxes the

actual date will vary from year to year. As at Yule, the Oak and Holly Kings battle, but this time Lord Holly, who presides over the waning Sun, should win.

A LITHA RITUAL

Some time in advance of Litha, choose two men, preferably equally matched, who can take the roles of Oak and Holly Kings. Yes, in the interests of equality you could nominate women, but the title King really does imply males. Give them plenty of advance warning and ask them to go away and practise their battle. This is important if you want to minimize personal injuries, as it should be thought of as a choreographed fight, rather than a real one. You will also need to consider what, if any weapons they are going to fight with. We favour staves, long pieces of wood that can be held with two hands spread apart. Fighting in this way is not about hitting your opponent, but rather forcing them backward to give ground, perhaps even unbalancing them so that they fall over. If you can also get them to wear suitable costumes, such as dark green (for Lord Holly) and light green (Lord Oak) tabards, that too is helpful. You will also need two crowns, one of oak leaves and one of holly leaves.

After the Sabbat Explanation the High Priestess should crown firstly the Oak King, saying:
 'This is the Oak King who reigns over the waxing Sun.'
 (It is important that the crown is secure on the King's head.) She turns to the rest of the group and says:
 'All Hail the Oak King.'
 Everyone repeats: *'All Hail to the Oak King,'* three times.
 The Holly King (uncrowned) steps forward to challenge Oak:

'Your time is over, you are old and past your best. It is time to make way for my youth and strength. For I am your brother, Lord Holly, and my time is now.'

The Oak King replies:

'I am the Oak King and I will not step down for you my brother. You seek the crown, then you must first prove yourself, and take it, if you can.'

The two Kings then proceed to battle, the rest of the group should give them plenty of space, but should also shout and cheer them on. Once Lord Holly has defeated the Oak King, he should remove his crown and return it to the High Priestess who then crowns the Holly King with the other crown, saying:

'To the victor the crown. This is the Holly King who presides over the waning Sun. He has challenged and fought bravely and he has won. But let everyone remember that Lord Oak is still with us and as the Wheel of the Year surely turns he will once again have his chance.'

She turns to the group and says:

'All Hail to the Holly King.'

The group, who will have gathered round again, repeat:

'All Hail to the Holly King,' three times.

The Holly King and the High Priestess then perform the Rite of Wine and Cakes, with Lord Oak standing to her left.

This really is an outdoor Ritual. However, if you have concerns about holding the whole of your Ritual outside you can have only the actual fight in the garden and the rest of the Ritual in the house.

Some other ideas:

★ *A Waterside Ritual.* If you are fortunate enough to have access to a secluded beach, then this is an ideal time to work beside the sea. It may at first seem that Lammas, being warmer, would be better, but in August most of the good locations are taken up by families on vacation. You can take the above Ritual and stage the battle at the water's edge, so that the defeated King gets a thorough soaking! But do ensure they both have something dry to change into afterwards.

★ *The Dawn Vigil.* Or as one of my Covenors once put it 'the yawn vigil', as at this time of year the Sun rises at around 3.30am in the UK! Just as at Yule, you can rise early (or stay up all night) to greet the Sun.

LAMMAS

Lammas, Lughnasadh, or Loafmas, falls on 1 August, and marks the first of the harvest and hence is a time to give thanks. In times past a volunteer would be selected as King for the day. He would be given the best of everything his heart desired and would lead the whole village to the cutting of the first field of crops. You can see the remnants of this tradition in the corn dolls which are still made at this time and in the gingerbread men, who used to appear only at this time. However, both these traditions have now lost their ties to the season.

This is also a festival of Lugh the Celtic Sun God. Lugh has been betrayed by his wife and slain by her lover. However, he does not die but is transformed into an eagle and later restored by his uncle Gwydion. Lugh is another of the dying and rising Gods. The theme of sacrifice to make payment to ensure a successful harvest is very strong at this Sabbat.

A LAMMAS RITUAL

One of the most fun, if rather messy, ways of enacting the Lammas Ritual is to make a Corn King to be sacrificed. This can be as small or as large as you wish, although do note that the larger the King the more corn you will subsequently have to clear away. Corn can often be obtained through garden centres or larger florists. Otherwise try to find a farm and ask the farmer's permission to take some. Don't just help yourself as this is neither socially nor magically acceptable.

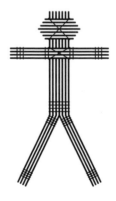

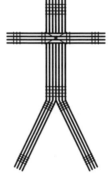

Make your King by dividing the corn into 4 mini-sheaves. As shown opposite two should be tied into one bundle from the top to half way down for the head and body, and from there they should be tied separately to make the legs. One of the others is tied and placed across the body to make the arms. The last mini sheaf is then folded and added to the head to make it rounder, and tied in place. The corn tops should stand up at the top of the head, like hair. Get as many Covenors as possible to help make the Corn King, as this emphasizes the sacrifice of their energies. It's best to make your Corn King outside, and sufficiently in advance for you to have more than one go, if it's your first time! If you wish you can thread seasonal flowers around his head for a crown and to make his features. Find a cloth to cover your King. On the Altar, and perhaps around the Circle, you can have some seasonal flowers and fruits. Instead of cakes, for the Rite of Wine and Cakes, you might like to have a loaf shaped as a wheat sheaf.

After the Sabbat Introduction everyone stands in Circle, with the Corn King being kept under his cloth behind the Altar. The High Priestess stands before the Altar, facing the group, and says:

'This is Lammas, the first of the Harvest, now we see all around us the signs of the bounty of the Great Mother. Let us all voice our hopes for the coming season.'

She then steps forward to the middle of the area, turns and faces the Altar and says:

'Let the land be fruitful, let the needs of all be met. Blessed Be.'

Then each person in turn steps forward and asks for three things; one personal, one for someone they know, and one for the Land in general. For example, to complete a personal project, for success for a friend's new course of study, for the safety of the habitat of an endangered species. After each person states their hopes the High Priestess and everyone else say together:

'Let the land be fruitful, let the needs of all be met. Blessed Be.'

When everyone has taken their turn the High Priestess says:

'We give thanks to the land and to the Mother Goddess and the Father God, whose bounty sustains us. But to truly give thanks we must sacrifice, not just of our time and our thoughts but also to repay the earth.'

The High Priest steps behind the Altar and brings out the Corn King, removing his covering cloth. The High Priest says:

'Here is the Corn King, symbol of the coming harvest. The King that sacrifices his life for the land and for the good of all. All Hail the Corn King, Lord of the Harvest.'

He walks around the Circle stopping in front of each Covenor who greets the Corn King:

'Hail to the King.'

Once everyone has greeted him the High Priestess steps forward and says:

'Before we take we must learn to give. The first of the harvest is the time of sacrifice and therefore we must give to the earth before we reap of her bounty. The time of sacrifice is now.'

At this point the High Priest lays the King upon the ground, on the sheet which was used to cover him, and everyone steps forwards and plunges their Athames into him. Care should be taken that only the Corn King is stabbed; the idea is that he should be slain, not that anyone else should be injured! Some of the Altar wine should also be sprinkled on him, to represent blood. Once he has been slain the High Priestess says:

'The King is slain, that the harvest might be fruitful, that the land and the people should thrive, from season to season and from year to year.

Blessed Be.'

The Corn King is then covered with a second cloth, and carried reverently from the Circle. The group chants:

'Hoof and horn, hoof and horn, all that dies shall be reborn. Corn and grain, corn and grain, all that falls shall rise again,' three or more times.

The Rite of Wine and Cakes is performed, but instead of cakes the Lammas loaf is consecrated and then broken up. Each person takes a little of the bread.

If you can, the Corn King should be burned and his ashes scattered to the winds. Alternatively he can be buried, but try to do this in such a way that your neighbours or any other outside observers do not think you are concealing a corpse!

Some other ideas:

* *The Corn Loaf.* If the prospect of making a Corn King, not to mention the amount of mess slaying him will make, deters you, then you might like to make your King from bread. Instead of stabbing him, everyone can tear off pieces which are then placed on a plate to be used in the Rite of Wine and Cakes. As an adjunct to either this or the above version the poem John Barleycorn can be recited, with different members of the Coven taking separate verses.

* *The Dying and Rising God.* This is similar in outline to that in the Oestara section above. For this Ritual the High Priest and High Priestess enter the Circle as the God and the Goddess. They dance and kiss, then the High Priest as the God falls to the ground where he is covered by a dark cloth. Then the High Priestess as the Goddess dances around him while the men drum and clap and the women sing. At first the pace is that of mourning and then, the tempo of dancing, drumming and singing quickens to resurrect him. When

she deems the time is right the High Priestess lifts the cloth from the High Priest and raises him to his feet, and again they dance together. If you have an even pairing of males and females in your group then this can be enacted by several couples in turn until each Priest has been 'reborn' by his Priestess.

MADRON

Madron, or the Autumn Equinox, occurs around 21 September. It is a time when day and night are equal, before the days become shorter than the nights. This is the time of balance in preparation for the resting period of winter. Here, at the height of the harvest, we should be looking at whether we have paid for what we have, and will harvest. Have we repaid our debts to the land, the Goddess and the God, to our friends and those around us? As a time of preparation for the resting period of winter this is a time to rid yourself of the unnecessary and

unwanted; to finally lay to rest old arguments and quarrels; to dispose of old guilt, envy and other unwanted feelings; to banish anything that might hold us back. This is the time when things should be put back into balance before the winter, lest nothing survive. It has been said that in times past this was the season when prisoners were released back to their homes and tribes.

A MADRON RITUAL

It is a good idea to give your Covenors plenty of time to think about this Ritual. It centres around identifying what you have been given, whether by others or by the Goddess and the God, whether tangible or otherwise, and what you have done, or need to do, to repay this. In this time when advertisers and the media encourage us to focus on what we do not have and what is bad in the world, I find that even experienced Witches sometimes forget the simplest but best of gifts: sunshine, health, new interests, friends, the love of their children or pets, progress in the Craft, the fellowship of the Coven, or even the goodwill of their High Priestess! It is also easy to think of repaying debts as being in terms of goods and money, rather than in terms of time and effort spent. If granny has been there to do the babysitting then, rather than buying a bunch of flowers, why not help her clear her garden in preparation for winter? If your best friend helped you through a crisis, then rather than a pint in the pub why not offer to help them bath their dog? If the Old Ones aided you in your magic then perhaps you can repay them by joining a tree planting programme?

You may find that you want to give your Covenors some help in preparing for this Ritual, perhaps during a training session (see Chapter Eight, Developing the Coven, for more on training Witches). Everyone should be encouraged to think of as many things as possible for this Ritual, for it is a way of clearing the decks for winter. Ideally, they should try to ensure that they repay as many of their

debts as possible in advance of the Ritual, so that the Sabbat itself is an affirmation of what they have done, rather than leaving them with a long list of what they have not done.

Once everyone has arrived for the Ritual, give them each several slips of paper and get them to write the things they have to give thanks for on one side and the ways they have repaid these, or intend to repay these on the other side. If they have other 'debts' to repay, or other unfinished business, such as unresolved quarrels, or old guilty feelings, they should treat these in a similar way. They are to take these slips of paper into the Circle with them. In the centre of the Circle have a cauldron, or other fireproof vessel, with an unlit nightlight in it. If you do not have a suitable vessel then, instead of burning the slips of paper, they should be torn into several pieces and kept until they can be burnt, buried or scattered safely later.

After the Sabbat Introduction, the High Priestess steps forward and says:

'At this time of balance we seek balance in ourselves. It is time to ensure that we can approach the dark part of the year with clear minds and hearts. We should resolve all quarrels, repay all debts, and release the prisoners of our hearts and minds, to set ourselves free for the resting time.'

She lights a taper from the Altar candle, approaches the Cauldron and says:

'I light this flame that it may take from us those things we have finished with (she lights the candle in the cauldron) and leave us free to move on in our lives. Blessed Be.'

She steps back. One by one each person places in the fire the slips which represent completed business. Note that uncompleted 'payments' should be kept aside until they have been dealt with. The High Priestess then steps forward again and says:

'The Goddess and the God will take these things from us and, even as we strive towards balance, will send us their energies to do so. What will each of you give them in return? Be careful what you offer here, for the Gods expect us to keep our promises to them.'

Each person now steps forward and expresses what they intend to do to honour the Goddess and the God. This can be taking on a new line of study in the Craft, working towards helping the land or the people in their Circle or community, or some other task that they will dedicate to the Goddess and the God. Have someone make a note of each of these promises as they are made. When everyone has finished the High Priestess says:

'I call upon the Old Ones to accept our offerings and to give us the strength to fulfil our promises. Blessed Be.'

The Ritual now moves on to the Rite of Wine and Cakes.

Some other ideas:

★ *The Dance of Parting.* This is the last festival in the Wheel of the Year with the Goddess as Mother and the God as her consort, as at Samhain they both take on their dark aspects. In keeping with the theme of balance, a Priest can be selected to be the God and a Priestess to be the Goddess. Choose a theme which allows them to also represent two complimentary opposites, and dress and/or mask them appropriately. We find that having the Priest represent the Sun and the Priestess the Moon works well, but you could easily select day and night, summer and winter, and so on. They enter the Circle and dance together Deosil, in a spiral dance, until they reach the centre of the Circle. Here they take their leave of each other and each dances their own dance three times around the Circle, making sure that they are moving further and further away from each other, before leaving the Circle, one to the East and one to the West. Whilst this dance of parting is going on the others sing and clap to accompany them.

★ *The Harvest Festival.* As this is the feast of the height of the harvest as well as a time of balance, you can combine these themes and bring offerings to the Circle. These can be for sharing around the group, or you can make up gift packages to give to others who you feel might appreciate them. Those Covenors who are skilled in making things might want to consider making gifts, preferably of seasonal items, to give out.

As you can see, there are recurrent themes which run through the Sabbats, many of which are interchangeable from one festival to another. It is not necessary to hold the same Ritual year in and year out, nor to have a new theme every time. So long as you, and your Covenors, are aware of the meaning behind the Ritual, and are in tune with that meaning, then your Sabbats will reflect the Wheel of the Year. Personally, I feel that it is important to have everyone take part in a meaningful Ritual which brings them closer to the Craft. Keep your Ritual to a reasonable length, as newcomers in particular find it hard to maintain focus and concentration through lengthy and over-complex Rituals. Also, be wary of setting your sights too high, especially in the early days of running a Coven; save more complicated ideas until you are sure of the capabilities of your Covenors. Nothing is worse than a flamboyant Ritual which falls flat because everyone is more concerned about how they appear than about the meaning of the Sabbat.

To repeat my earlier point, generally speaking Esbats are working Rituals, whilst Sabbats are celebratory Rituals. This is not to say that magic cannot be performed at the Sabbat, indeed these are times of great energy which can be utilized to great effect, but for the purposes of this book I have talked about the Sabbats in their celebratory state only. Should you wish to incorporate magical workings then they should take place after the Sabbat's specific Rites, and you can easily make the appropriate changes yourself, remembering to include the actual casting of the Circle.

DEVELOPING THE COVEN

s I've said before, one of the better definitions of a Witch is Healer, Teacher and Parent, and at no time are the latter two more obvious than in guiding the progress of the individuals in the Coven.

One of the reasons people seek to join a Coven is to find out about the Craft from those with practice and experience. They want to be taught Witchcraft. As High Priestess you are the person they look towards to provide this teaching. Of course, we do not actually teach people to be Witches in the same way as a teacher educates in the classroom, we act as mentors and facilitators and assist them to become what they are capable of. I believe that just about everyone has the ability to be a Witch and for many it is more a question of remembering than of learning. All the High Priestess needs to do is to help them to unlock the door(s) to that memory. In the Craft it is up to the student to seek to learn, not the High Priestess to push them. Having said that, it is a good idea to have some idea of how you are going to guide their development and lead their learning. If you are blessed with great organizational abilities and a phenomenal memory, then you will be able to do this in an informal way, without notes and records. If,

however, you are like me, then you are going to need to develop some kind of structure to work to, and keep some kind of record as to progress.

In this chapter I am going to look at Covenors in four categories, and for each one I am going to set out what I feel they should know and understand before being ready to move on to the next. These 'levels' are not fixed in stone, they are guidelines. I always adjust the way I work to suit the individual, their interests and the rate at which they can take on new ideas. Each Covenor will be slightly different, some may be great at visualization and hopeless at recalling information. Some may be naturals at healing magic, but struggle with any form of herbal work. You have to look at each individual, listen to what they are saying and develop a pace which works for them. This cannot be done on a 'one size fits all' basis. I shall also look at some of the problems you may encounter in this development process, and ways around them. In addition to this I am also going to look at the kind of Coven records you might want to keep, and their purpose.

So, what are these four groups of 'trainees'?

* *Aspirants*, those who have not yet taken their First Degree Initiation. Here you are looking at ensuring that they understand what the Craft is about, effectively trying to make sure that they really have made an informed choice, and also preparing them to join the Coven proper.
* *First Degrees.* From First to Second is the time of the High Priestess's maximum input into the growth in learning and understanding of Initiates.
* *Second Degrees* should be far more pro-active in their learning and hopefully will be coming to you for guidance rather than instruction.
* *Third Degrees.* Here you are supporting the new High Priestesses and High Priests through the early days of running their own Coven. And hopefully, receiving feedback about their experiences which you, in turn, can use to refine your techniques.

In this chapter I will give suggestions for the teaching of each group, but please remember that you will also need to judge each individual's learning at their own pace. Similarly, the suggestions in each section are not supposed to be rushed, but rather spread out over the period of that level. But before I move on to the specifics of each group I'd like to talk a bit about Books of Shadows.

BOOK OF SHADOWS

Every Witch or aspiring Witch should keep their own Book of Shadows. It is a journal or record of their workings; what they did, when, how and why, what happened, how they felt, what the results were. It can also be used to keep notes of dreams, recipes, ideas, etc. Some traditions, especially Gardnerian, encourage Witches to copy from the Book of Shadows of their Initiator. Others prefer each Witch's Book of Shadows to be theirs alone. The Book of Shadows has two main purposes: first, it is a record of magical workings which allows the Witch to look back and see what worked well and what didn't. In the fullness of time, they have notes from which to design their own Rites and Rituals, and to help them run their own Coven. The second purpose is as a record that the High Priestess can access so that she can see how well the student is progressing. She can tell whether her explanations and exercises are working, and, if necessary, adjust her techniques. For me the keeping of Books of Shadows is one of the fundamentals to Coven membership, although it is also one of the hardest disciplines to get some Covenors to stick with, but more of that later.

A BOOK OF SHADOWS SHOULD CONTAIN:

★ The date of the Ritual, working, etc.

★ Phase of the Moon, the time of day, and the day of the week.

★ The purpose of the Ritual or working.

★ What was actually done.

★ Thoughts and feelings about the Ritual/working.

★ The results of the working. These may have to be added later when you know how well the magic worked.

★ Notes taken during any training, lectures, talks, workshops, etc, relevant to the Craft, and thoughts and feelings on these.

★ Any other information the owner feels relevant to their Craft experience.

IT SHOULD ALSO:

★ Be written clearly. Some High Priestesses insist that it is handwritten, not typed or placed on a computer. Note that nothing kept on a computer is secure, even after it has been deleted!

★ Be written up as soon as possible. Ideally at the end of each Ritual, working, etc.

★ Be available to the High Priestess whenever she asks to see it. This means bringing it, fully written up, to each and every meeting, unless she specifies otherwise.

★ Be kept safely. A Witch should guard their Book of Shadows and prevent it being seen by any other than their High Priestess and/or Initiator.

A BOOK OF SHADOWS MIGHT ALSO CONTAIN:

★ Seasonal Observations. Some Witches like to make notes on what is happening in the natural world around them. When plants are coming into bud, flower and fruit, etc. The variations in activity of the birds and animals and even the changes in activity of their pets.

★ Herbal planting details. Those who have a herb garden might also like to record when seeds were planted, including the phase of the Moon, and the results of their growth.

★ Herbal recipes. They may also keep notes on any herbal lotions, potions and recipes they make, and the results of their use.

★ Results of Divination. Those practising a form of divination such as the Tarot, Runes, etc, might like to keep records of their readings, what cards or stones came up, their interpretation and how this actually manifested in life.

★ Dreams. Many Witches like to record their dreams and possible interpretations in their Book. Some like to confer with their High Priestess on possible interpretations and also record her thoughts.

★ Notes on Private Studies. Sooner or later most Witches will explore a topic outside of the range of formal training, and can keep notes and records of this too.

★ Thoughts on the Craft. Even simple musings and thoughts on the Craft may be recorded in the Book of Shadows. Mine also contains odd quotes from books, radio and the TV which I feel may be pertinent to the Craft, the Coven or even to my writing.

A BOOK OF SHADOWS SHOULD NOT:

* Contain information which would reveal the identities of any of the participants, ie full names, addresses, etc.
* Contain information which reveals the location of workings. (These 'do nots' are intended to prevent exposing the Coven or its members, should the unthinkable happen and the Book get lost.)
* Be written in code, unless this is previously agreed! As High Priestess, you will need to be able to read it.

EXCUSES FOR NOT COMPLETING:

Newcomers to the Craft, or indeed to the idea of keeping a Book of Shadows, are understandably reluctant to do so. They feel nervous that they won't do it right, that you will mark it like their teachers used to at school. They feel that their hand-writing will be scruffy, their spelling poor and their grammar inadequate, and that they won't say the 'right' things. You will need to reassure them that you are not interested in these aspects, only in their development within the Craft. For these reasons it is a good idea to make your first check on Books of Shadows as early as possible. They may also resent the idea of having to do some kind of 'homework', in which case you need to point out the reasons for keeping their records.

In my time as a High Priestess I think I have heard just about every possible excuse for not completing a Book of Shadows. The following is just a selection, along with some replies you might want to consider. Alternatively, you might simply show them this list as a deterrent!

* I don't have the right book – 'Any book will do.'
* I don't have the right pen – 'Any pen will do.'

✴ My computer's broken – 'Do it by hand.'

✴ My printer's broken – 'Do it by hand.'

✴ I don't know how to start – 'Just start, it'll soon come.'

✴ I don't know how to stop – 'Continue until you've said all you need to.'

✴ My dog/cat/hamster/goldfish ate it – 'You're supposed to keep it safe!'

✴ My husband/child/parents, etc might find it – 'If you cannot rely on your near
and dear not to look into your private affairs then you will need to find a safe
place.' I have allowed the occasional Covenor to leave their Book at my house.
Another method is to incorporate the Book of Shadows into another book
which conceals its identity, but this is not foolproof.

✴ I don't have time – 'Are you sure you have time for the Craft? Make time!'

✴ I hurt my hand – 'You can dictate your notes to me.' It's surprising how many
injuries can be cured by this statement!

✴ I've never done it before – 'Now's a good time to start.'

✴ I have already done it before – 'Then you'll know what to do!'

✴ I don't see the point – Reiterate the reasons.

✴ Why can't I just copy yours/Fred's? – 'Because these should be your thoughts
and feelings, not mine or Fred's!'

✴ I bought a printed book – 'Oh, was the author present at your Rituals and
workings?'

✴ I've lost my book – 'Find it! And start a new one in the meantime.'

✴ I left it on the bus – 'You did what!!'

You can see from these that the reluctance to complete Books of Shadows develops a lively imagination in some Covenors! However, there is a bright side; nearly all Witches who have kept their Book of Shadows for a year or more are really glad they did so. Some will even thank you for staying on their case. There is, however, one category of people you will need to be a little more tolerant with, and that is anyone genuinely suffering from dyslexia, or who cannot write.

However, even in these circumstances, Covenors can often be helped to produce some form of short notes to keep a record. Use of a diary means dates do not have to be written, Moon phases can be drawn rather than written, and in severe cases, a series of ticks and crosses can give a sense of how they feel. The reason I do not excuse anyone from keeping a record is that I have found that often a person will overstate their writing problem. Also I have had one non-writing mature Witch who found that this gave her the impetus to go away and finally learn.

So, having persuaded your Covenors to complete their Books of Shadows, and hand them in to you, what are you looking for? Well, as I said above, you are not there to mark grammar, spelling and punctuation. The only spellings you might like to correct are those of Deity names, festivals and the like, and then, bearing in mind that many of these have differing spelling, only if you are sure that they have got it wrong. You are certainly not there to tell them what are appropriate thoughts and feelings to have, or write down. What you are checking is that they have the facts, like dates, moon phases, etc, correct. You are also looking to see how they reacted to what was done, so that you can adjust your methods to increase their understanding. You can also make a partial assessment of a person's commitment to the Craft, by the care and diligence with which they write up their Book! Occasionally I feel moved to make a comment or suggestion in someone's Book, but I only ever do this on a post-it note so that they can write it in if they wish, or remove it if they prefer.

By the way, most Witches do not end up with one Book of Shadows, but rather many volumes. Unless you have very tiny handwriting, and a very large book, you are almost certainly going to end up with a series of books which reflect your progress in the Craft.

ASPIRANTS

In the chapter on selecting new members I talked about some of the things that you will be looking for in an Aspirant. Here I shall be talking about some of the knowledge you will want them to acquire in the period before their First Degree:

* ✦ What the Craft is really about. They need to understand the differences between what they have been told about the Craft, whether negative or glamorous, and the reality. They need to know the difference between Witchcraft and Satanism. They need to know the difference between Witchcraft and Buffy, Sabrina, etc.

* ✦ In order to truly choose the Craft as their path, they need to have an idea of the difference between Witchcraft and other belief systems. For this reason many High Priestesses will ask Aspirants to look at one or two other religions.

* ✦ They should understand and accept the beliefs of the Craft (see Chapter One for a summary of these). This may sound obvious, but unless you are prepared to talk to them about it, and listen to their thoughts and feelings, you cannot be certain that they have really accepted these tenets.

* ✦ They should understand and accept the secrecy of the Craft and the Coven. Most people do appreciate that their fellow Covenors may have good reasons for not wanting to be 'outed'. A rare, stubborn few have to have it impressed on them that to give this information away can really adversely effect their fellow Covenors and means they will immediately be asked to leave the Coven. These few may also need to actually have it pointed out to them that talking in the supermarket queue, on the bus, at a Pagan or Craft event, or

elsewhere where there might be other people around, is just as bad as taking an ad out in the local paper!

★ If you intend to have them take a Coven Oath they should understand the meaning of that Oath.

★ Similarly, if attending Circle they will need to know how to behave in Circle. This includes, but is not limited to: not putting anything on the Altar which has not been authorized by the High Priestess, eg coffee mugs, ashtrays; always walking Deosil in Circle; focussing on the Ritual and no private conversations, side chat, and so on.

★ If your Coven wears robes, then you might want to encourage them to get or make theirs. Don't forget to give them some guidance, otherwise they might well turn up with the lemon yellow, sequined and feathered variety!

★ They should obtain their Athame. It is customary in some groups that the first thing a First Degree Initiate does after Initiation is to consecrate their Athame. Of course if you prefer to encourage your Aspirant to attend Circle, or to work magic, you should consider having them consecrate their Athame sooner.

★ They should have a reasonable understanding of the nature and meaning of the eight Sabbats.

★ I also require each Aspirant to select one of the tales of the Goddess and the God, to learn it and to be able to discuss not only the story, but its relevance to today's world.

★ It is a good idea to get them to start their Book of Shadows, even though they may not be attending Rituals, as this gets them into the habit of committing their thoughts and feelings to paper. I insist on this and make it one of the requirements to be met before taking the First Degree.

★ You may want to consider a complete or partial ban on magical workings at this stage, unless they take place with your advance consent. Most people, when they first discover the Craft, are eager to start with magic. However, unless they are 'a natural' they will have little self-discipline and control. Too many times have I been asked to sort out a magical mess created by an over-enthusiastic Aspirant, or even a First Degree Witch, who has decided that they can go it alone!

★ Probably most importantly, they should know who to turn to when they need help, and to understand that, when starting out on a new path, there are no 'stupid questions'. In other words, they should be encouraged to ask, ask, ask!

Now, whilst I have said that in the Craft learning should be student-led, with the Aspirant you will need to set the guidelines and standard for this. In these early days it is often a good idea to try to set regular meetings so that you can assess their progress. There's more on organizing 'training' sessions later in this chapter.

BETWEEN FIRST DEGREE AND SECOND

The period from First to Second Degree is the time when you will be most involved in deciding what the Initiate learns and in guiding them. As the First Degree is about self-knowledge and understanding I tend to assign a number of tasks directly related to this, as well as more general Craft-related subjects. Most of us come from backgrounds where we are encouraged to focus on our weaknesses. Even being aware of our strengths, let alone speaking of them, is considered somewhat rude and arrogant. As a result we develop a poor and inaccurate self-image. Furthermore, we are constantly bombarded by images of what we should look like, how we should act, and what we should own, which further erode our self-confidence. As self-understanding can only come from self-honesty, and that includes owning up to your good points as well as your bad, it's obvious that some work in this direction is going to be useful.

✸ The new Initiate is asked to write of (at least) 20 things they like, and 20 things they dislike about themselves. I then go through these list with them. I often find that the dislikes will include a number of things which are cultural or media-generated stereotypes. For example: men who say they are too sensitive; women who say they are too forceful. Not to mention the ubiquitous too fat, too thin, comments from perfectly normally-proportioned men and women! While we all have 'problem areas' in our personalities, and sometimes shapes, it is important to recognize the difference between a real problem, and a 'standard' which is imposed by the outside world. The likes list can be just as interesting, as many people give themselves credit for habits and attributes which are not necessarily good for self-confidence. For example: people who are part of a domestic partnership but who are always the one to do the shopping in their lunch hour, or rush home from work to cook the family supper; individuals who spend every moment of their spare time helping out their friends, to the neglect of their own lives and families. This can be a difficult discussion as many people prefer to hang on to their preconceptions rather than admit to a need for change. It is worth pointing out to them that an effective Witch is personally honest, and strives towards balance.

✸ Any Witch who was not required to complete a Book of Shadows during the Aspirant stage really should start one now!

✸ During the First Degree Initiation you showed them the tools of the Craft. During their time as a First they should learn to use these and also be encouraged to make or seek their own. Most Witches find that these come to them during this year anyway. Many tools can be made; however, I do not recommend novices trying their hand at metalwork unless they can find skilled tuition. The prospect of an Athame or Sword parting company from its handle, possibly at speed, during Circle is quite a frightening one!

- ★ A First Degree Witch should know how to behave in Circle, if you did not complete this instruction during the Aspirant stage.
- ★ They should know how to create the Sacred Space: blessing and consecrating the elements on the Altar; calling the Quarters; inviting the Lord and Lady, and Casting the Circle.
- ★ The new Initiate needs to understand the phases of the Moon, not only when they are but what they relate to and what kinds of magic are more appropriate at different phases.
- ★ They should also be learning tales of the Triple Goddess to add to their understanding of the divine, the Lunar Cycle and the Wheel of the Year.
- ★ As with the Aspirant stage, you will need to maintain some control over non-group magical workings. In my Coven, First Degrees are still required to contact me before working on their own. They are not supposed to gather in sub-groups to work magic and they are not allowed to work at the Dark of the Moon. This is not because I want to spoil their 'fun', but rather because as High Priestess I feel responsible for making sure that their magics are effective, and do not back-fire, leaving others to work overtime to sort out unnecessary problems.
- ★ Visualization is the key to the Craft. Around 10 per cent of new Witches have or acquire the skill easily. For around 50 per cent of Witches it comes fairly naturally with a bit of practice. The other 40 per cent will experience varying degrees of difficulty, and some can take many years to really grasp the technique at all. But visualization is the way to make the magic work, it is the way towards understanding of other people, it is the key technique to learn. There are a great many exercises which can be practised to develop this skill, many of which start by using visual recall. Start off with simple exercises: visualizing their home, and sketching out a floor plan; visualizing a loved one, and what they were wearing on a particular occasion; Kim's game, where a number of objects are placed on a tray, observed for a minute, then the tray is covered and the subject has to describe everything on the tray.

Once the aspect of visual recall has been re-awoken you can start to take it a step further. Storytelling is a simple way of doing this, and they can practise at home, listening to radio plays, or talking books. Another method is listening to the television with eyes shut, only opening them to see how well they have visualized the scene they heard. These exercises might sound simplistic but they not only help to develop visualization skills, they also increase observation skills, another key element of the Craft. When you are happy that they have grasped the essence of these techniques you might want to move on to guided visualizations and pathworkings. These are effectively stories where the listener becomes the subject of the story, in other words they visualize that the tale is happening to them. A pathworking differs in that, at some point, the narrative pauses and the listener experiences sights, sounds or feelings which are theirs alone. The story is told with the listener, or reader, as subject, ie 'You are walking through the woods on a Moonlit night …'

First Degrees may also have ideas about what they would like to learn, and this is to be encouraged as we are still talking about 'student-led learning'. The more the individual suggests and contributes, the more they are taking personal responsibility for their own development. Occasionally you may have to temper their enthusiasm, or divert them back on to the path of the Witch, but this should be the exception rather than the rule. Very occasionally I have needed to give someone 'time out' to pursue a particular subject, especially where this involves outside instruction such as evening classes, eg an Aromatherapy course. In these cases I try not to delay the next initiation, but the individual must be as ready as any other First Degree, before they can take their Second.

SECOND TO THIRD DEGREE

By this point your Initiate should have an understanding of most of the techniques and principles of the Craft. Of course they will still need practice in carrying them out to become competent but the foundations should be there. During the period between Second and Third they should be ready to start explaining these techniques to those who are coming after them. At this point your involvement in their own development will be more along the lines of suggesting areas of study, and guiding them towards reputable sources of information. Having said that there are still some things you may wish to approach more formally:

⭐ Writing Rituals. Even if you have a set list of Coven Rituals there will always come a time when you need to cover a slightly different topic, or approach a subject from a different angle. In these cases you have to write a new Ritual, and it is only sensible that you start to guide your initiates in this skill before it becomes essential. To give you an example: recently I was asked to assist a High Priest in writing a Male Mysteries Rite. Now even as a fairly experienced High Priestess, being female I've obviously had a distinct lack of personal involvement in Male Mysteries Rituals! However, understanding of the structure of Ritual writing, knowledge of the stories of the Gods, and assistance from an experienced High Priest friend of mine, have enabled me to give advice which I trust will be useful.

⭐ Creating their own magic and spells. Again you may have a series of Coven spells, but sometimes everyone needs to create a spell from the ingredients to hand rather than from a tried and tested list in the Coven book.

★ I rarely find it necessary to place any embargo on magical working on to Second Degree Witches, as by this point they are usually aware of the benefits of contacting me first. Not least because they will know that I will lend magical aid to them for their workings.

★ I mentioned above that the Second Degree is about passing knowledge on as well as gathering it. Having said that, I do not expect the newly-initiated Second Degree to immediately start training Aspirants and First Degrees. In the early days they will sit in on 'training' sessions and be expected to contribute. It is only when I feel they are ready that I will suggest that they take one person to the side to give instruction on a particular aspect of the Craft, eg creating the Sacred Space.

★ The Second Degree should also be seeking out and choosing their own areas of specialization. The following are just a few of the areas of individual study that your Second Degree might choose to examine: herblore; incense making; candle making; metalwork, eg Athames and Swords; homeopathy; Aromatherapy; first aid; local Deities and energies; Sacred Sites; tales from a particular pantheon; the Tarot; rune readings; the Ogham; divining rods; astral projection and travel; working with a familiar; lotions and potions; wine making; writing chants; creating dances, and so on. They may also choose to supplement their Craft learning by more formal external study, for example: a branch of medicine or nursing; massage; counselling; psychology; ancient languages; animal welfare; geology.

Basically the lists can be endless, as nearly every aspect of life is part of the world of the Witch. It is not intended that everyone should study everything, but each Witch should be encouraged to explore those areas which interest them. Not only is this beneficial to the individual, but as the Coven's overall spread of knowledge grows, there is the opportunity for everyone to benefit from sharing that knowledge.

AFTER THIRD DEGREE

The Third Degree presumes that the initiate is ready and able to run their own Coven, and therefore theoretically needs no guidance from their High Priestess. The newly-created Third wants to feel independent, wants to prove that they can manage on their own, and wants their High Priestess to feel proud of them. They don't want to feel supervised, overlooked, or that you are waiting for them to make a mistake! At this stage, however much you point out that you are there to guide, advise, or just to be a shoulder to lean on, they will want to make their own way. All you can do is ensure that the lines of communication are kept open, so that when they need you they feel able to approach. Give careful consideration to whether you want to present the newly-made High Priestess with copies of your Rituals. On the one hand it does give them a head start, and save them work, on the other hand it can stifle creativity. Only you will be able to judge whether this is a good thing by your knowledge of the individual.

It is usually a good idea to keep the two Covens and their Covenors separate, at least until such time as the new High Priestess has truly found her style and made the new Coven her own. This prevents the new High Priestess, and group, from feeling overshadowed in any way, and allows each group to establish itself as a separate entity.

ORGANIZING TRAINING

There are many ways of doing this: you can meet with each and every Covenor individually; you can organize training sessions by level; you can hold all-in group sessions. You can also use the telephone and/or internet as your training ground, or to supplement group workshops. All of these have advantages and disadvantages. However, the first and foremost consideration has to be your time, as an overcrowded schedule will not only take over your life but will have effects on those you are seeking to bring along. I know of a Coven which at one time had four meetings a month plus Sabbats and informal sessions, not to mention specialist training for a couple of members. Assuming your Coven meets at every Sabbat and Esbat, you already have 21 meetings a year to co-ordinate (8 Sabbats plus either 12 or 13 Esbats depending on the cycle of the year), so before you commit yourself, give some serious thought to how much more you can sensibly fit in before it becomes a burden not only on you, but on those you live with. Over the years I, like many High Priestesses, have tried a number of combinations and thus far one of the most workable I have come up with is as follows:

- ✯ Aspirants are dealt with individually. I, or a senior representative of the Coven, meet with them once a month or thereabouts, in an informal setting. We discuss areas of the Craft and endeavour to answer their questions, while also assessing their compatibility with the Coven. Towards the end of their year and a day they may be allowed to one or two Rituals, but their 'training' takes place away from the rest of the group.
- ✯ First and Second Degrees, and any Thirds who wish to, meet once a month at the New Moon where we hold training sessions. These sessions usually take

the form of about one hour of general discussion on a topic of the Craft before the group is then split up so that experienced Seconds and any Thirds can give Firsts guidance on specific topics. This leaves me free to have one-on-one discussions with each person in the group, although pressure of numbers sometimes means that not everyone will have that opportunity every month. The structure of these New Moon meetings will vary according to the number of people and their progress to date. It sometimes happens, where we have had no new entrants for a while, that the whole group is quite experienced, in which case I will ask other Covenors to talk on one of their areas of expertise. Alternatively, we might hold a New Moon Ritual at this time.

★ Anyone who feels they would like a particular topic discussed is encouraged to put it forward as a suggestion for a future New Moon. Where an individual raises a topic which I don't feel is appropriate for the whole group, generally something very specific to that person, I will arrange a one-on-one meeting with them as soon as I can. This applies particularly to Seconds with questions about their specialization(s), and Thirds with enquiries about their own Covens or Covenors.

★ Everyone in the Coven who is on the internet, and has secure access, is also encouraged to use that as a question and answer forum, although I do point out that if it is urgent they should telephone, in case I can't or don't collect my email. However, email is an excellent forum for the explanation of many points of interest, but it is no substitute for direct contact.

★ Occasionally, special meetings will be held for senior Covenors, where we discuss the running of the Coven and other matters which affect it as a whole.

★ At least once a year I hold a social evening, where the Craft is not discussed, but to which non-Craft partners, and perhaps Aspirants, can be invited. This is partly to allay the fears of partners who may worry that we are weird or scary, so that they feel they can contact us if they wish. It also means that we can better get to know each other in our non-Witch roles. One of two of these

parties have been afternoon affairs held at the weekend so that children can attend too.

This still gives quite a full schedule as the 21 meetings have now grown to 33 (8 Sabbats plus either 13 Full Moons and 12 New Moons or vice versa), plus a number of one-on-one meetings with various people. Whilst it is good to delegate much of the work involved in this, it is important that not only do you have over-all control, but that you are seen to have it. Otherwise, you can find that the Coven is heading off in a direction which was not your intent, and that your more junior Covenors keep their mentors informed rather than yourself.

COVEN RECORDS

As mentioned above, unless you have a really good memory, you will need to keep some kind of Coven records. How much information you need to effectively run your Coven will depend to a certain extent on you, however it is worth men-tioning that security of this information is a priority. The following are some of the items I, or other High Priestesses of my acquaintance, have found useful, and some of the ways I have chosen to discreetly record them.

★ *Covenors' personal details.* Obviously you will need to have their name, address, phone and email details. The best place to keep these is in your normal address book, not under C for Coven, but with each person simply appearing as a normal entry. To this you might like to add birth date, so that greetings can be given or sent as appropriate, or you can enter this in your diary. Do not add Witch names here!

⭐ *Dates of Esbats and Sabbats.* The easiest way to keep track of these is to use a diary which includes moon phases, and then add the Sabbats and other meetings yourself. There are one or two diaries and calendars on the market which list not only the Moon phases, but also Sabbats and seasonal festivals for other belief systems too. The latter can be useful for planning forward dates if any of your Covenors come from a multi-religious household.

⭐ *Attendance records.* You might like to keep a note of who attends, who was absent without a good excuse and who is off regularly because of sickness. It might sound harsh but occasionally you get someone whose inability to attend has less to do with any underlying condition, and more to do with an excess of social life! If you think you can keep these notes safely in your diary, fine, otherwise you might like to make a tick-list, perhaps noting each person by a single initial.

⭐ *Who took which roles in Ritual.* If you are assigning the different roles within Circle on a rotational basis, then you may need to make a note of who did what at each Ritual, otherwise some poor soul may never get to Cast the Circle or will be forever calling the element of Fire. Notes will help you make sure everyone gets to try everything. I tend to assign roles according to level and ability, thus giving individuals something to aim for. Hence First Degrees will call quarters, Second Degrees might cast the Circle or invite the Goddess and the God. More senior members will perform the Rite of Wine and Cakes. Again you can use a coded tick-list for this.

⭐ *Skills and abilities.* From time to time I subject my Covenors to a questionnaire which lists a large number of Craft-related skills and abilities. Each individual then rates themselves as to whether they: can teach the topic; understand the topic; wish to learn the topic. This is of more use in a large Coven as it is generally easier to keep track in a small group.

⭐ *Dates of Initiation and Witch Names.* In the early days of a Coven it can be easy to remember these, but as time goes on, and numbers rise, it can sometimes be hard to keep track, especially where more obscure Witch names are used. Again, unless you are certain that your records are entirely secure you will need to develop some form of shorthand or code.

SECURITY OF RECORDS

The difficulty with keeping any kind of Coven record is that you must be certain that they will be totally secure. I know that I am making something of an issue of this but, as High Priestess, you do not want to be the one responsible for allowing details of the Coven to be accessed by anyone. This includes other Coven members, as nothing will destroy group trust as fast as having it known that you cannot keep personal information secure. Most of you reading this will not have a huge problem, but for the one or two who live with people who can't bear not knowing, the following may help:

★ Don't use a computer hard drive. Even if you live alone, or only share access with your working partner, you cannot guarantee that it will never break down and have to go away for repair. Remember, even deleted files can be resurrected. Also, be very wary of storing information only on a floppy disc or CD ROM, as it could either be found by someone else, or crash at the most difficult moment.

★ If you live alone, or in a household where your privacy is respected, a diary is probably the most convenient format for storing information. But do be careful to put it safely away all the time. It's not unknown for a visiting relative or friend to help you to check a date by opening your diary for you. Besides, a diary is such a temptation to even the most conscientious person.

★ You can of course develop your own code, meaning that even if found your notes will be unreadable. The only drawback is that dedicated snoopers will either see this as a challenge or will ask you outright what it's all about!

★ There are any number of devious hiding places for books and papers, but probably the most effective way to conceal books is amongst other books. Just ensure that the spine is neither tempting, nor a give-away! One of my Covenors used to secure her Book of Shadows by keeping the notes in wallets in a loose leaf folder, hidden between pages of recipes cut out of magazines. Note, though, that this will only work if the concealing subject is one you are considered likely to be interested in!

TIPS AND HINTS

There are a number of simple techniques you might want to consider which can make life a little easier when you find yourself in the role of mentor:

★ *Speed Reading.* Some people can read very quickly, and still retain the meaning, others find they need to proceed slowly and perhaps make notes. As High Priestess you may often be asked to recommend books, or be lent books which your Covenors think are interesting. Unless you read fast you can find your time taken up reading books that perhaps don't interest you personally. However, there is a way of quickly assessing a non-fiction book to see if you really want to read the whole thing. First, read the cover and introduction; here the author will usually give you an idea of what the book really contains. Next, read the first and last paragraph of each chapter, bearing in mind the chapter title. This should give you a flavour, not only of the book as a whole

but also of which are the most interesting chapters. Now you are in a better position to see if you want to read the whole book. Where a Covenor suggests or recommends a book, ask them to identify which they think are the most interesting bits, before you accept it.

★ *Book loan and return.* Many High Priestesses accumulate quite a large selection of books on the Craft, and their Covenors may ask, or need, to borrow them. Most people are good at returning borrowed books; some, however, absent-mindedly hang on to them forever! Here are some ways of ensuring that your books come home. Put your name in it. Only lend for a specified period of time, and only one book to a person at a time. Make a note of who borrowed what and when. If a book returns in a dog-eared, ragged manner tell the offender that this is not the way you like your property treated; don't let it pass, otherwise you could end up with your whole collection looking like the dog's toys! The lending of books is always fraught with difficulty but the bottom line is: if you can't bring yourself to ask for a book back, don't lend it!

★ *Difficult questions.* Every so often you will be asked a question that you don't know the answer to. Just occasionally you'll get someone who likes to put you on the spot so that they can show off their expertise. In both these cases there are a couple of ways of sliding graciously out of the firing line. If you think back to your school days you may remember this phrase, 'That's very interesting, come back and tell me what you find out,' or you can try, 'That's quite subjective, what do you think?' In other words, get the student to do the work. Alternatively, go for the honest approach: 'I'm not sure, I'll try to find out,' but don't commit yourself to extensive enquiries and research unless you are sure you have the time. Also be aware that some questions may well be fascinating to both the enquirer and yourself, but they may not be relevant to either the Craft or your Coven. By all means satisfy your curiosity if you wish, but not at the expense of getting on with what you need to do.

✦ *Praise and Criticism.* Although most people will try their hardest, there will still be times when you need to redirect them or address their misconceptions. It is not only difficult to receive criticism but also to give it, and to a lesser extent this also applies to praise. When you are giving praise don't just say, 'That's great,' show that you really have been paying attention by being specific: 'I really like the way you did ..., it shows real understanding,' or, 'Your piece on ... really made the Ritual meaningful for everyone.' When you do have to correct someone, try to do so in a constructive manner: 'It might have been easier (quicker, simpler, more effective) if you had tried ...' Try to sandwich criticism with positives: 'Thank you for writing the Blessing. It might have been less wordy if you had omitted the bit about the ancient Romans, but it was very effective and really invoked the spirit of the season.' Always try to avoid personal criticism, generalizing and bias: 'Your problem is that you never pay attention. I'm surprised your mother put up with you,' is personal criticism and not at all conducive to an ongoing relationship. Don't generalize by saying, 'That's typical of a man (fire sign) to build the fire too big.' Whatever your experience, don't be tempted to target any one group in your comments, it isn't amusing and you may well offend the quiet one in the corner. Try to avoid saying things like, 'So and so forgot to bring the wine so we can't trust her with anything else.' Once you label a person as a failure you can actually inhibit their success.

Finally, two really important points. First, praise should be given in front of the group, criticism is better delivered quietly in private. Secondly, never, ever be tempted to criticize one group member to another, or to join in with discussion of an individual's personal faults. To do so will destroy the group's trust in your ability to be just and fair. In fact, if you find this kind of behaviour is going on, even in jest, then you should call a swift halt to it as it can be very divisive to the group as a whole.

- ★ *Tackle minor issues.* If you make a point of dealing with minor issues as they arise you stand a good chance of averting larger problems. Make a gentle comment the first time someone is late, or talks over you, and they may well not do it again. Leaving it until that person has done it so often that you are thoroughly irritated may cause you to have an unnecessary argument, and possibly to pick on other people who unwittingly copy that behaviour. A mentor of mine once said, 'Never let a person get away with stepping on your toes, it's only two paces to your throat!'

- ★ *React to undercurrents.* Where you sense that all is not well, or feel that something is going on that you are not a part of, make a point of finding out. Don't wait for it to come to the surface, as by then it could be too late to deal with easily. Probably the only exception to this approach is mutterings which take place in the week or so before your birthday, as you never know!

It would be easy, when reviewing the above, to get bogged down in the details, so it is important to remember that these are ideas and suggestions intended to make it easier to structure your Covenors' development. The key to organizing this is to allow yourself to be flexible; don't commit months in advance to specific dates and schedules, as then you will leave no room for addressing things which come up over time. Remind your Covenors regularly that *they* are expected to come to *you* with their questions, suggestions and ideas. You are not supposed to be force-feeding them or chasing them up. If they don't want to progress that is their concern, not yours.

NINE

THE LIFE CYCLE OF A COVEN

The following are some definitions which you may find useful to refer to when reading this chapter:

Solitary A Witch who works alone.

Partnership Two Witches who work together, frequently, but not always; a couple who are partners in daily life too.

Coven Three or more Witches who regularly work together.

Mother Coven The Coven that the High Priestess came from and/or the Coven from which the new Coven descends.

Hive Off Where one or more Witches from the Mother Coven set up their own group, with the blessing of the High Priestess of the Mother Coven.

Daughter Coven The new Coven, directly descended from the Mother Coven.

Training Coven A group which will take on newcomers, subject to compatibility, etc.

Whilst every High Priestess sets out with the intention of running a Coven which will serve the Craft well and will endure, sometimes the Goddess organizes life so that things don't quite work out as planned. Some Covens last, others come and go. Some Covens remain seemingly unchanged, others move more rapidly through different sizes and styles. It used to be that a Coven, once established, would find its style and remain that way, with few changes, for many years. These days there are many variables which can intervene with the 'plan'. Here I'm going to look at some of the ways that a Coven can grow, how it might change or shrink, and some reasons why a Coven may close.

A COVEN WILL GENERALLY START IN ONE OF TWO WAYS:

★ A 'Hive Off' from the Mother Coven. A Priestess, on getting her Third Degree, or sometime after, will be encouraged by her own High Priestess to start a Daughter Coven. The new High Priestess will probably also be encouraged to take a couple of members of the Mother Coven with her, in order to give her a basis from which to build.

★ A Solitary Witch, or a couple of Witches, who have not been able to find a Coven to join, will found their own. Sometimes, this can actually happen unintentionally; a couple of Witches practising together find themselves joined by a third and then a fourth and before you know it there's a Coven.

A COVEN WILL TEND TO
DEVELOP IN ONE OF TWO WAYS:

* Very rapid growth. This often happens when a Coven starts in an area where there previously was none, especially where the High Priestess has taken the decision to actively seek members (see Chapter Four, Finding Coven Members). Rapid growth has its good and bad points. On the one hand, there is an initial period of frantic activity, but at least this takes place when the new High Priestess is full of enthusiasm and energy. On the other hand, it is easier to make mistakes in selecting new members as you haven't had time to develop your own system for weeding out the less likely candidates! Very rapid growth is often followed by a steep learning curve for all concerned and quite frequently leads to at least a partial 'boom and bust' scenario, which is discussed later in this chapter.

* Slow growth. If you keep a low Coven profile and are not actively seeking new members then growth is likely to be slower and will give you the chance gradually to develop your own style. It can have the disadvantage of requiring changes in rules and policy as you go along. The guidance, organization and control needed with four or five Witches is totally different from that needed when you have a dozen or more.

After the initial days in the life of a Coven things usually settle down and allow you to focus more on the beliefs, ritual and magic of the Craft. You should find that you now have enough time to explore interesting avenues of knowledge and to refine skills and abilities; your own as well as those of other people. If you have managed to organize your Coven so that you have a spread of people at different levels, you may also find that you can delegate some of the tasks and responsibilities, giving you the time to take an overview and consider the direction you want the Coven as a whole to move in. Sometimes, you can be so busy actually doing

the work of the Coven and the Craft that things become 'samey', and you find yourself working the same style of magic and Ritual over and again, because you don't have time to explore new techniques and ideas.

DAUGHTER COVENS

Assuming all has gone well with your Coven you will have steady growth and will find yourself Initiating to the Third Degree. At this time you will want to give some thought to whether it is time to establish a Daughter Coven. Generally speaking, the most important factors in this decision are:

★ *Numbers.* If your Coven has got to the stage where you can't all reasonably fit into your working space then you need to consider a Hive Off. Sometimes you may even have to consider this before you are ready to give the new High Priestess her Third Degree, in which case she will be the Acting High Priestess, and you will need to oversee the Daughter Coven as well as your own. Conversely, if you only have five or six Covenors in total, then splitting the group may not be practical. If the new High Priestess is very keen to start her own Coven then this may be the time to suggest that she actively seeks new members whilst using the Mother Coven as a base until she has enough newcomers to make her own Coven viable.

★ *Willingness.* However much you may feel that the new High Priestess is ready to form her own Coven, you cannot force her. By all means encourage and prompt, but do be aware that some people can't run a Coven, perhaps because of personal circumstances, perhaps simply because they are just not ready yet.

✭ *Ability.* This shouldn't be a factor in the decision as you shouldn't be giving the Third Degree to someone who is not capable!

SOME OTHER CONSIDERATIONS IN THE ESTABLISHMENT OF DAUGHTER COVENS:

✭ *Geography.* It used to be said that the new Coven should not be based within 3 miles of the original, so that there were not two groups working in the same population. In these days of high population density, this is less of an issue. Besides, people will either seek out the Craft or they won't, and you might have 30 or more potential Witches in a small town and only a couple in a large area. The only thing you will need to bear in mind is that the new Coven will need to either find its own outdoor working site, or co-ordinate use of the existing one with the High Priestess of the Mother Coven.

✭ *Support of the new Coven.* As mentioned before, the new High Priestess will need at least some support, if only in terms of another High Priestess to let off steam with! However, this does mean that you don't want to be founding too many Daughter Covens in a short space of time. Give yourself the time to be certain that each new High Priestess is coping well, before establishing the next.

✭ *Allowing autonomy.* Having said that, you need to allow the new High Priestess enough freedom to develop her own style. Support does not mean interference or control. The new High Priestess may well choose to do things you wouldn't, or which you have tried and seen fail, but she must be allowed to make her own choices and perhaps even some mistakes, otherwise she will not be able to grow and learn.

✭ *Two distinct groups.* It can be quite important to prevent comparisons between the two groups, otherwise you can end up with some Covenors feeling that they should be allowed to pick and choose who they work with, or that they can swap from one to another to suit their social lives. Not only can this be highly disruptive but it prevents each Coven from maintaining its own style. At its worst you can end up with the two High Priestesses feeling as though they have to compete to have the most exciting or enjoyable Coven. For these reasons, contact between the two Covens should be minimized until the Daughter Coven becomes established.

LOSING MEMBERS

There are many reasons why people might leave a Coven:

* The individual finds that, after all, the Craft is not for them. There is nothing to do here other than to wish them well and remind them to please keep the secrecy of the Coven and Craft.
* The individual finds that Coven working in general does not suit them. There are some people who really are happier as Solitaries. It may be that they need greater flexibility in order to fit their Craft around their family and work. It may simply be that they would prefer to work on their own. Again, you need to do nothing other than wish them well and, if you wish, offer to be a contact and support should they need one. You may also wish to extend an invitation to attend some or all of the Sabbats to this person, if you feel that it will not disrupt the other Covenors.
* The individual feels that this is not the right Coven for them. Sometimes you will get a Covenor who feels they would like a different style of Craft, perhaps more formal, or more relaxed, or does not feel in tune with the Coven for any

one of a number of reasons; some good, some not so good. I have had a Covenor who disagreed with my running of the Coven on the grounds that I was not the most physically attractive woman in the group! Here you can simply let them go, or if you are in a position to do so, recommend them to another Coven, if you know of one. This latter action should only be attempted if you are certain that they will be an asset to the other Coven: don't knowingly pass on a liability!

★ The individual moves away. While there is a school of thought which says that the Craft should come first in every Witch's life, I believe that we owe it to the Goddess and the God, as well as our partner and children, to do our best for our family. In this case you should send them on their way with your best wishes, recommend them to another Coven if you can, and offer them such support and contact as is practical until they find their feet in their new location.

★ The individual has a personality clash with another or others in the group. This most frequently happens when they have been in a relationship with another Covenor and there has been an acrimonious break. As High Priestess you are not there to judge who is right and who is wrong in such circumstances, even if this were really possible. One potential solution is to make both parties spend some time away from the Circle, in the hope that time will allow feelings to die down. Otherwise, you will either have to hope that one party chooses to leave, or make a choice that you are prepared to stick to.

★ The individual disagrees with the High Priestess on an important issue, eg discipline. It is one thing for your Covenors to question you on aspects of the Craft, it is quite another to allow them to question your judgement or to subvert your position. Where possible you should attempt to resolve this on a one-to-one basis, otherwise you will need to send them on their way. Even the most talented High Priestess will not be able to run an effective Coven if she has someone determined to undermine her.

★ The High Priestess feels the Coven would be better off without this individual. In this case you have to very carefully examine your own motives: just finding this person a bit of a challenge is not really good enough. If, however, they are disruptive, seem to be using the Craft for the wrong reasons, are offensive to other Covenors, etc, then yes, it really is time to let them go. The best thing to do is to meet with them, explain your problem and see if they have any real solution. Obviously, you are less likely to have problems of this kind if you make a point of dealing with small issues as soon as they arise, before they can become big ones! If you are not satisfied that they can reasonably adjust, then your decision has to be final. Try to deal with this in as kind a way as possible, after all, you want to avoid having someone vengeful hanging around the edges of your group. You will also need to communicate your decision, and your reasons, to the rest of the Coven, so that they understand why you took the action you did. It is also a good idea to ask your Covenors not to discuss this amongst themselves unless they are prepared to include you in the discussion, just to prevent people getting carried away by misconceptions.

This may feel like it's all bad news, but please be reassured that problem people are few and far between, it's just helpful to have thought it through before you have to! Neither are you likely to have many people leave your Coven, although, like buses, these things do sometimes seem to run together. The main thing to remember is that it is better to have a small, effective and happy Coven, than a large one with problems.

BOOM AND BUST!

This is a phenomenon which sometimes happens. The Coven grows and develops quite satisfactorily, and then for no one reason it rapidly shrinks, losing nearly all of its members. While this is usually just the way the cards fall, there are a number of potential causes you might like to look out for:

★ Being too relaxed about bringing in newcomers. Whilst a stable Coven is a joy to work with, there can come a time when stagnation sets in. A Coven with a through-flow of newcomers arriving and High Priestesses and High Priests moving on to found Daughter Covens might be more work, but it does retain its freshness and enthusiasm. It's not as though you should be looking for newcomers every week, but perhaps you should start to feel some concern if it looks like being a year since your last Aspirant.

★ Being too fussy about potential Aspirants. When you have an established Coven, especially if you've had to deal with one or two less than wonderful Covenors, it is easy to become over-particular when selecting new entrants. If you feel you might be heading this way, try to recall how some of your more effective Covenors appeared to be when you first met them, warts and all! This category also includes Covenors being too protective about the status quo. Sometimes the Coven collectively feels more comfortable without the 'bother' of starting afresh with newcomers. Again, you need to consider this possibility, otherwise you can end up with no-one ever being 'good enough'!

★ Poaching. If you find that several people are leaving, and seem a bit diffident about really explaining their reasons, you might like to consider whether someone else is trying to attract your Covenors away. This is rare, but does

sometimes happen. If you have good communication with your Covenors then you should hear about anyone who seems to be taking more than a passing interest in them or the Coven. The most obvious warning sign is someone who seems to want to talk to your Covenors, but never seems to want to talk to you.

★ The hidden troublemaker. There are some people in this world who are never really happy unless they are promoting trouble for others. A typical example is the person who tells one person just enough about a given situation to ensure that they are concerned. They then tell someone else a similar, but slightly different, tale. They then sit back to watch the ensuing 'fun'. Often these people are positive that they are only trying to help, but basically anyone who spends all their time minding other people's business for them is a potential troublemaker. They are usually very difficult to spot because they are not actually part of the tale, nor are they involved in the subsequent misunderstanding, but trust me, they'll be hovering on the sidelines! One of the hardest lessons to learn, both for a High Priestess and for her Covenors, is not to listen to second-hand news. It is rarely accurate, and often causes more trouble than the actual root cause of the so called 'problem'. One of the worst examples of this I have come across was a Covenor who decided to tell the rest of the Coven their High Priestess was heading for a nervous breakdown, and furthermore that it would be best if she was 'not bothered' by the other Covenors. Before the High Priestess had actually got to the bottom of this, most of the Coven was in disarray, several people had left, and the troublemaker had not only managed to make herself appear a wonderful person, but was also putting in a pretty good bid for a Coven take-over.

★ Underlying dissatisfaction, usually aggravated by the High Priestess being cut out of the communication loop. As your Covenors grow they become able and willing to take on more responsibility, and mostly this is a good thing. However, as the above tale illustrates, do take care that your Covenors always

come to you first with their problems and worries. As soon as you allow someone else to become the first point of contact then you have opened the door to communication missing you out completely. However busy your schedule, you do want, and need, to know how each and every member of your Coven feels. Ideally, your Covenors will always feel that they can approach you direct, but there will always be one or two who 'don't want to bother the High Priestess'. Equally, your Covenors should always be prepared to tell anyone who approaches them in this way that they 'really should talk to the High Priestess first, she doesn't bite'! If, at any time, you sense that there might be some kind of undercurrent, make a point of having a quiet talk with everyone on an individual basis. And don't be afraid to ask the question, 'Is there anything about the Coven or the Craft which is bothering you?' Yes, you may get a lot of trivia, but you may also be just in time to prevent a niggle turning into a problem.

SOME OTHER KEY EVENTS IN THE LIFE OF A COVEN

★ The High Priestess is temporarily unable to fulfil her role. Accident and illness can happen to anyone. Normally, someone else will be able to step into her shoes and keep things running smoothly in the interim. This person should keep the High Priestess up to date on what occurs where this is possible, or should fully update her when she returns. When she returns, the High Priestess should endeavour to have a quiet word with each of the Covenors in order that they can be reassured that she is indeed still concerned about them, and can tell her how they fared in her absence.

✴ The High Priestess becomes pregnant. There is no reason why a pregnant High Priestess should not continue to run her Coven. She may feel that it is not appropriate for her unborn child to be present at certain Rites and Rituals, in which case she will need a stand-in while she sits outside the Circle maintaining her presence and authority. She might feel more comfortable if she performs a spell of protection for her child before entering Circle, but rest assured the Goddess and the God are not going to harm an unborn child. Towards the end of pregnancy, or if there are any concerns, she may also wish to sit out the more energetic aspects of Ritual, especially circle dancing! After the birth, there is still no reason why she should not continue in her role – I often had my baby son parked just outside the Circle, even when we worked outside. Of course, once a child becomes aware, and especially mobile, it's much better for everyone if a babysitter is used, or the child is firmly asleep before everyone arrives.

✴ The High Priestess moves away. In an ideal world this needn't happen, but High Priestesses have to live in the real world too. They may be required to move because of family responsibilities, or to maintain their income. Usually, there is someone in the Coven who can take over, possibly on an 'Acting' basis if they do not yet have their Third Degree. There is no reason why the outgoing High Priestess shouldn't stay in close contact with the Acting High Priestess until she is fully capable of managing on her own.

✴ The Coven is closed or disbanded. Very rarely a High Priestess will decide to close or disband a Coven. When this happens it is a sure sign that something has gone seriously wrong. I know of only two circumstances where this has happened. The first was deemed the only way to rid the Coven of some troublemakers, who if evicted would almost certainly have caused problems. The Coven in question was reformed as soon as a discreet period had passed. The second was where the Covenors were only interested in the Craft if someone did it for them. In other words they were seeking a Priesthood/

congregation relationship and were not at all interested in personal responsibility and self-development.

The ways in which a Coven changes over time can be as varied as the Covenors within it, indeed more so. There is no right or wrong pattern of growth, and sometimes no obvious reason for the most startling of events. As a High Priestess you will work to have the best possible Coven. You will try to be parent, healer and teacher to this assortment of individuals, to understand their concerns, soothe their fears and help them to solve their problems. You will try to provide them with an enriching environment in which to study the Craft and to make the most of their individual talents. However, as a human being you will need to recognize that you can only prepare yourself so far and try to do your best. Sometimes you will need to be pragmatic and accept that life doesn't always go exactly as planned or worked for.

TEN

THE GOOD COVENOR

The bulk of this book has been addressed to the High Priestess who is, or is thinking of, running a Coven, although I trust it also gives everyone an idea of the complexities involved. This chapter is directed towards those who would join and work in a Coven, because without enthusiastic and committed Covenors no Coven can function or survive. The first step towards being an effective Covenor is finding the right Coven.

FIND THE RIGHT COVEN

Many people, when they first discover the Craft, want to find a Coven to work and train with. However, although the Craft is growing rapidly, there are still not all that many Covens who are taking on new members. Those that are around can be quite hard to find. As a result the newcomer often feels that they must join the

first one they come across, whether it fits or not. Not only that, but it can be quite hard to tell whether a Coven is right for you, until you have had at least some experience of it. From the opposite point of view, the High Priestess will want to ensure that newcomers fit in well with existing Covenors and that they will be comfortable with the way the Coven works. These are just some of the reasons why there can be what seems a lengthy introductory process before a newcomer is allowed to join the group. There are some things the potential Coven member can do to ease this process:

★ *Be honest.* When asked questions about yourself and your interest in the Craft don't try to give the 'right' answers, give honest ones. Experienced Witches can always sense if you are not being absolutely truthful, even though they may choose not to say anything, and it definitely makes them more than usually cautious. Also, if at any point you have any doubts about the Craft or the Coven, talk to the High Priestess. Again, she will sense if you are trying to hold something back.

   If you feel the need to take someone with you to your meeting with the High Priestess, especially in the early days, please tell her. It can be really uncomfortable to know that someone is watching you without knowing why! Not only that, but she might like to introduce herself to help reassure that person.

★ *Be patient.* It can be hard to put your enthusiasm on hold if it has taken months, or even years, to find a training Coven. However, being keen is one thing, but being pushy is more likely to alienate the High Priestess than to impress her. Remember that while joining the Coven may seem to be the most important thing in your world at the moment, the High Priestess will have a whole host of other concerns and activities to juggle.

★ *Be timely.* As it says above, you are not the only item on the High Priestess's agenda. Being late for meetings, or not turning up at all, will not do your case any good whatsoever.

★ *Complete any tasks or exercises.* It may seem pointless, for example, to read a book on Islam, but you may be asked to do many things which at first seem unconnected with Craft. The High Priestess will have her reasons, she just may not choose to tell you yet. If you cannot complete a task, or have any questions, talk to her as soon as you can.

★ *Be discreet.* If you have read this book, or others like it, you will be aware of some of the reasons why not all Witches want their interest in the Craft to become public knowledge. However great your enthusiasm, avoid telling your friends that you're off to meet a Witch, brandishing books on the Craft, or discussing the Craft in public. You may not know the High Priestess, but you could well be surprised at how much she'll be told about you, and your activities!

If you want to grow in the Craft and reap the benefits and rewards of Coven life – personal development, self-respect, greater control over your life, and more – it is important that you not only apply yourself but also become an effective Covenor who actively contributes to the Coven. There are two types of people in any team: leaders and followers. It is as important to have good followers as good leaders in order to make the team function. Likewise, in the Coven it is important for the Covenors to understand what is expected of them. In fact, it is good Covenors who make a good Coven. Obviously it is up to each High Priestess to decide on what she requires from her Coven members, but some things are pretty much held in common:

REGULAR ATTENDANCE

There is little point in joining a Coven unless you are prepared to commit to attending its meetings and Rituals. This might seem obvious, but a surprising

number of people join a Coven and then fill their diary at Esbat and Sabbat dates with their social engagements. If you really feel that these are more important than the Coven then perhaps you should reconsider your membership, and look to working as a Solitary. Everyone will have the occasional immovable fixture in their diary, but those committed to the Craft will try to schedule as much as possible around the Coven dates.

It is the Covenors' responsibility to keep in touch with the High Priestess to confirm dates, not her responsibility to phone round every Covenor to remind them. This means that you make one phone call, rather than the High Priestess having to face a huge phone bill.

Oh, and if for some reason you can't attend, please let her know. This avoids either delaying the Ritual for someone who isn't coming, or a mass panic because you fear something may have happened to a latecomer who didn't get in touch.

PUNCTUALITY

Pagan Mean Time may be a joke in some circles, but for the harassed High Priestess it can be a real problem. Being late is being rude; not only are you implying that your life is more important than everyone else's, but that it is more important than your Craft. While one individual may have the whole evening and night set aside for Ritual, another may have to consider getting home before the babysitter leaves, or charges overtime! There have been occasions when I have had to threaten regular latecomers with a 'lock out'. If you think you're going to be late, please let the High Priestess know, it saves worry about whether you may have had an accident on the way.

Being too early can cause just as many difficulties. Consider this: on the day of a Ritual I have to feed the family and get my son bathed, off to bed and asleep, before I can start moving the furniture and setting the Altar. If one or more

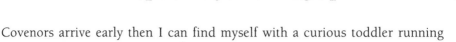
Covenors arrive early then I can find myself with a curious toddler running around wanting to join in the fun!

Oh and by the way, don't forget to go home! You may be able to sit up all night and function effectively the next day, but others may have an early start.

MAKE YOURSELF USEFUL

When you arrive at the Covenstead *ask* what you can do to help. Please do not presume, as there is nothing more irritating than finding that your carefully planned Altar has been rearranged by someone else. Even if you have travelled a long way, please do not expect your harassed High Priestess to rush around making you tea or coffee. Only too often have I seen (and in the early days I have been) the High Priestess running around getting everything ready, whilst the Covenors sit and chat, or prepare themselves for Ritual. After the Ritual or meeting ask what you can do to help clear up. Many a High Priestess finds herself with a mountain of washing up and heaps of partly-eaten food after the Sabbat celebration.

PREPARE FOR THE RITUAL/MEETING

Arrival at the Covenstead is not an opportunity to catch up on the activities of your fellow Covenors or the latest gossip; these issues can wait until after the Ritual. If you wear robes, get changed. If the Ritual is available for study, then study it. Otherwise, settle yourself and prepare mentally and psychically for what you are about to do. Even if you feel you are fully prepared, spare a thought for those who do need a few minutes' peace in order to cast off the stresses of the day.

KEEP YOUR PROMISES

The Coven Oath and Oaths of Initiation are not just words you say to get through the process, they are promises you make to the Goddess and the God. And please don't be one of those people who stick to the words of an oath, but spend all their time trying to get around its intent.

KEEP YOUR COMMITMENTS

If you have said that you will do, bring, or make something then either do it, and on time, or give your High Priestess as much advance notice as possible. She may be slightly irritated at having to find an alternative, but not nearly as irritated as she'll be if she only finds out on the night! However keen you may be to contribute, remember, slow to promise, quick to deliver.

PAY YOUR DUES

No-one much likes asking for money, even fewer enjoy pursuing a debt, and unpaid Coven subs are debts. Try to pay up willingly and on time. If you are short of cash, have a quiet word with your High Priestess, don't just avoid the issue.

WRITE UP YOUR BOOK OF SHADOWS

Second to chasing unpaid Coven subs I really dislike having to pursue people for their Books of Shadows. As you saw in Chapter Eight, I really have heard all the

excuses! Chasing Books of Shadows is tedious, time consuming, unnecessary and liable to raise the blood pressure of even the most generous-hearted High Priestess.

TAKE CHARGE OF YOUR PERSONAL DEVELOPMENT

If you want to grow in the Craft then you will have to do more than just turn up and go through the motions. You will need to read, to study, to practise and to look at acquiring new skills. Try not to go to your High Priestess saying, 'What do I do next?' Instead, try to develop some idea of which direction you would like to go in and say, for example, 'I'm interested in learning the tarot (herblore, or whatever). Where should I go from here?'

COMMUNICATE WITH THE HIGH PRIESTESS

One of the most annoying things for a High Priestess is finding that half the Coven consider that they have identified a problem and have set out to solve it without so much as trying to talk to the High Priestess. Resist the urge to 'spare her the extra work/worry', keep her in the communication loop. Some High Priestesses forbid contact between Covenors outside of Coven meetings to prevent this problem, and believe me, I have been tempted! If you have a problem, concern or worry, talk to your High Priestess *first*. She might suggest that you then talk to another Covenor who has expertise in this area, but this way she will know what is going on. This is not limited to Craft-related troubles, you can also go to her with your personal troubles too. High Priestesses are, on the whole, kind, caring and patient with their Covenors, unless and until they find that they are being circumnavigated. Oh, and by the way, if you feel unwell and not sure if you should attend, remember to contact your High Priestess and talk to her.

LISTEN TO YOUR HIGH PRIESTESS

First, it is the height of bad manners to talk over someone else. Secondly, you may well miss important information. But most of all, I mean listen, don't just let the words pass through your ears; pay attention. Then if you don't understand, ask.

TELL YOUR HIGH PRIESTESS ABOUT YOUR MAGIC

Most High Priestesses encourage Covenors to work magic at home. However, you really should inform your High Priestess first. In the early days she can advise you and perhaps prevent some of the more common errors or tortuous procedures. But in any case she will almost certainly offer her magical support (you don't have to be in the same room to work together), and if she feels it's appropriate she may contact and enlist the help of a number of other Witches. My coven has a world-wide network of contacts that we can call on for this purpose.

LOOK AFTER YOUR HIGH PRIESTESS

After reading this book you will be aware that the High Priestess does a lot of work to make everything happen. And, like the swan sailing serenely and paddling furiously, most of it happens out of sight. In addition to selecting Aspirants, writing and co-ordinating Rituals, supervising individuals' growth in the Craft, helping Covenors with their personal and Craft problems, etc, she will also have a personal life, work and family commitments, bills and so on. If she's well organized she may even have a social life too. Despite all this she will be available for you, to listen to your problems and worries, Craft and otherwise, to guide and advise you and generally be your mentor. But please do be considerate.

Phoning up at 2 am with a crisis is fine, phoning at midnight to check the content of next week's Ritual is not so great.

If she seems over-tired or harassed then ask what you can do to help, and be prepared to muck in with the less glamorous chores. Preparing for Ritual not only includes setting the Altar, it includes shopping for tea, coffee and candles, tidying, vacuuming and clearing the kitchen! It used to be a tradition that newer members of the Coven would visit the High Priestess regularly to do her housework; not such a bad idea now I come to think about it!

Don't save up your worries until just before Ritual, get in touch beforehand. If this is not possible then try to keep them until the Ritual is over. This doesn't include urgent concerns, such as a sick child who needs healing magic, so you will need to apply a little common sense.

If you are worried about your High Priestess, perhaps she seems preoccupied or unwell, then talk to her first, don't prejudge or make the mistake of thinking you know best what is good for her.

LOOK AFTER YOURSELF

You, the Covenor, are as important as everyone else in the Coven. Without Covenors the Coven doesn't exist. One of the key tenets of the Craft is personal responsibility, so take care of your physical, mental and spiritual health.

Don't be afraid to ask for magic to be worked on your behalf; it can be really frustrating for a High Priestess to discover that a Covenor has forgotten to mention their own problems.

Remember, one day you too might be running a Coven!

TERMS AND DEFINITIONS

S ome of the following words may have only been touched upon briefly in the text. However, they are words which are in common use in the Craft and may well crop up in other books you have read or will read. Other words are also in common use but have a particular meaning within the Craft, and that is the meaning I have given here.

Aspirant	A Person who has joined the Coven and has taken their Coven Oath, but has yet to take their First Degree Initiation. These are sometimes referred to as Neophytes.
Athame	The Witches' knife or blade. Traditionally a black-handled knife with a double-edged blade nine inches long, the Athame is used when invoking and banishing the elements and other energies. The only thing an Athame should cut is air, or the wedding cake at a Handfasting.
Besom	The traditional Witches' broomstick. On one hand this is a symbol of fertility which is literally jumped during a

Handfasting to signify the leap from one 'life' to the next. The Besom is also used to symbolically sweep the circle.

Boline The white-handled knife. This is the working knife of the Witch and is used whenever any cutting, say of herbs, or carving of symbols is required.

Book of Shadows A personal record or journal of all your magical workings, and the thoughts, feelings and results that come from them. Gardnerians refer to The Book of Shadows which was written by Gerald Gardner, together with some of his senior Coven members.

Candidate A person who wishes to join the Coven, about whom the High Priestess has yet to make a decision. Some Candidates may be Initiates where they have self-initiated, or in some cases the Initiates of other Covens.

Censer A heat-proof container for incense. A censer usually has a perforated lid, to let the heat and vapours out, and chains so that it can be hung from a convenient hook, or even swung so that you can circulate the perfume.

Chalice The Chalice is a symbol of the Goddess and can be made from wood, stone, glass or metal. It can be plain or ornate. What is important is that it contains the wine used in the Rite of Wine and Cakes, or in the Great Rite.

Circle This defines the Sacred Space of the Witch. It is created whenever and wherever it is needed. Casting the Circle is just one part of creating the Sacred Space. A Coven would traditionally cast a Circle nine feet across, however, when working on your own it should be as small or large as your needs.

Coven A group of three or more Witches (two would be a partnership). Coven size varies considerably, although some consider that a

'proper' Coven should be made up of six men, six women and the High Priestess. The Coven is the family group of the Witches.

Covenor — Any member of the Coven who has taken their Coven Oath, from Aspirant to High Priestess.

Covenstead — The home of the Coven, where most of the indoor meetings and Rituals will take place. The Covenstead is usually the High Priestess's house.

Craft — One of the terms for Witchcraft, which has been rightly described as both an Art and a Craft.

Daughter Coven — The term used for a Coven which has been formed by a member of the original Coven, and is hence directly descended from the Mother Coven.

Deity — A Goddess or a God. The term 'Deities' is often used generically for all Goddesses and Gods, wherever they have come from.

Deosil — Clockwise or Sunwise. When setting up and working in your Sacred Space you should always move Deosil, unless you are undoing something.

Divination — The techniques and ability to discover that which might otherwise remain hidden to us. The tarot, crystal ball, astrology, tea leaves and many others are all forms of Divination. Witches tend to use the term 'scrying', although strictly speaking this refers to the Dark Mirror, Cauldron, Fire or Witches' Runes.

Divine — A broader term than Deity, the Divine encompasses both the Goddess and the God and includes those aspects which do not have a gender or a name.

Elements — The term elements is often used to refer to Earth, Air, Fire and Water. However, it is important that the fifth element, that of Spirit, which we ourselves bring to the Circle, is not forgotten.

The elements are the keystones of the Craft and also refer to aspects of ourselves as well as energies around us.

Esbat	The Witches' term for Full Moon meetings or workings.
Goddess and God	The female and male aspects of the Divine. However, the term the Gods is often used to denote both.
Great Rite	This is the symbolic union of the Goddess and the God. Generally it is performed with the Chalice and Athame. The exceptions to this are between working partners and in some forms of initiation.
Handfasting	One of many Rites of Passage, Handfasting is the name for the Witches' wedding. It differs from most 'orthodox' kinds of wedding in that both parties enter as equals and make their own individual vows to each other. Handfastings can be of different prearranged durations.
High Priestess/ High Priest	The leader of a Coven is usually the High Priestess, she may lead jointly with her High Priest, but holds ultimate authority and responsibility. Some groups are run by the High Priest alone, usually where there is no female of sufficient experience to take this role.
Hive Off	The process where one or more Witches from the Mother Coven set up their own group, with the blessing of the High Priestess of the Mother Coven.
Initiate	An Initiate of any degree, including the High Priestess.
Initiation	Initiation literally means to begin. However, in the Craft, Initiation is seen as the permanent declaration an individual makes to their Gods. Many of the paths within the Craft refer to three degrees of initiation, each denoting a different level of attainment and ability.

Lore	Knowledge, handed down from generation to generation. Originally oral tradition, a lot of the old lore is now finding its way into books. Much ancient lore which was thought, in our scientific age, to be superstition, is now being proven and accepted.
Magic	The ability to create change by force of will. It is worth remembering that many things we take for granted, like electricity, would have been considered magic by our ancestors.
Mother Coven	The Coven that a High Priestess came from and/or the Coven from which a new Coven descends.
Occult	Literally, the word means hidden; in medicine 'occult blood' simply means blood that has been found through testing because it cannot be seen with the naked eye. Today, Occult is often used as a semi-derogatory term for anything which is not understood and is therefore feared.
Orthodox	A term I have used to identify those beliefs which people tend to think of as older than the supposedly new age beliefs, when in fact the reverse can be said to be true. For example, people tend to think that Christianity is an older belief system than the modern Pagan beliefs, when in fact the origins of Paganism (including Witchcraft) vastly pre-date it.
Pagan	This is a generic term for a number of pre-Christian religions; Druids, Witches and Heathens to name a few. Pagan probably comes from either the word *paganus* referring to those who didn't live in the towns (a version of country-bumpkin if you like!), or it may come from the word *pagus*, being an administrative unit used by the occupying Roman government. Either way it was originally used as an insult, now it is a 'label' worn by many with pride.

Partnership	Two Witches who work together; frequently, but not always, a couple who are partners in daily life too.
Pathworking	A Pathworking is a form of guided meditation in which you take a journey which leads to an opportunity to discover more than you already know. Sometimes also referred to as 'interactive guided meditation'.
Pentacle	This is a five-pointed star with the points touching but not overlapping a circle. It symbolizes the five elements together with the Circle of power. The Pentacle is worn by many Witches, but is also currently very fashionable, so you cannot be sure whether the wearer is of the Craft or not.
Pentagram	This is a five-pointed star not enclosed in a circle, which also symbolizes the five elements and, like the Pentacle can also be worn. However, the main uses of the pentagram are for invoking and banishing.
Priest and/or Priestess	In the Craft we are each our own Priest or Priestess, and need no-one to intercede with or interpret our Gods for us.
Quarters	The four cardinal points of the compass; north, south, east and west, which are linked to the directions of the Elements.
Reincarnation	To believe in reincarnation is to believe that we return to this world many times, as many different individuals.
Rite	A small piece of ritual which although complete in itself is not generally performed on its own, such as the Rite of Wine and Cakes. A series of rites put together make a ritual.
Rites of Passage	These rites are specific to marking the change from one stage of life to another, such as birth, marriage and death. Their names in the Craft are Wiccaning, Handfasting and Withdrawal. These names are different from those in general use, which reflects the different emphasis that Witches place on these events. There are

other Rites of Passage but they are less common even in the Craft today.

Ritual	A series of rites put together to achieve a specific result.
Sabbat	A seasonal festival. There are eight Sabbats in the Witches' calendar which together are often referred to as the Wheel of the Year. Sabbats are traditionally times of great celebration and festivity. Many of the old Sabbats are still celebrated, under more modern names; for example, Yule is known as Christmas, and Samhain as Halloween.
Sacred Space	For many religions their place of worship, or religious centre, is a building. Witches create their Sacred Space wherever and whenever they need it, and their magical workings, and some of their celebrations, take place within its boundaries.
Scourge	A form of ceremonial whip. It represents the sorrows of life and can be used in some forms of Initiation and discipline. It is generally made from a short piece of wood with several lengths of ribbon or silk attached to one end. When used it should be felt by the subject but should not mark them. The Scourge has been used in power raising but this is not recommended.
Scrying	The Witches' term for Divination, especially when carried out using a Dark Mirror or the Witches' Runes.
Solitary	A Witch who works alone.
Spells and Spellcraft	A spell is a set of actions and/or words designed to bring about a specific magical intent. Spellcraft is the ability, knowledge and wisdom to know when, as well as how, to perform such actions.
Strong Hand	For a person who is right-handed this will be their right hand, for someone left-handed it is their left. The strong hand is sometimes called the 'giving hand'.

Summerlands	The Witches' name for the place our spirit goes to between incarnations, where we rest and meet with those who have gone before us, and where we choose the lessons we will learn in our next life.
Thurible	Also sometimes called a Censer, this is a fireproof container designed to hold burning charcoal and loose incense. Unlike a 'true' censer, it does not have to have either a lid or chains, as it is intended to sit on the Altar.
Training Coven	A Coven which will take on newcomers, including those with no experience of the Craft, and actively encourage them to learn, grow and develop in the Craft.
Visualization	This is seeing with the mind's eye, so strongly that it appears no different from 'reality'. Visualization is not just about seeing, though, as when you are skilled at it, all your senses will be involved. For example, when visualizing the element of Air you will feel the wind touch your hair and skin, hear its passage through the trees and smell the scents of spring. Visualization is one of the key factors in working the Craft and performing magic.
Wand	A piece of wood the length of its owner's forearm. In some traditions the Wand is only used where the Athame is not; in others the Wand and Athame can be interchanged.
Wicca and Wiccan	Wicca has been largely adopted as a more 'user friendly' term for Witchcraft. Personally, I do not describe myself as a Wiccan as it simply leads to the question, 'What does that mean?' You will sooner or later end up using the word Witch. Some people consider that those who call themselves Wiccans are less traditional than Witches.
Widdershins	Anticlockwise, and the opposite to Deosil.

RECOMMENDED READING AND POINTS OF CONTACT

There are a great many excellent books available today on the Craft. I have not tried to list them all here but have selected some of those which I have found useful. This might be in a general way, or because they specialize in a particular area which is too complex to be covered in an all-round text. Many of these books are intended to be used as reference, rather than to be read as literature. If a book is not listed here it does not mean it is not a valuable work, nor is it intended as a slight to the author. Equally, not every book here will suit every reader, as each has his or her requirements in terms of content, and preferences when it comes to style. If you find yourself reading something you find tedious or 'heavy going', do not feel that you have a problem, it may simply be that you and that work are not compatible. You might like to try the 'speed reading' technique mentioned in Chapter Eight, page 185. You may find some of these books are out of print, however, it should be possible with perseverance to locate them through the library system. In any case, I would always recommend trying to get hold of a book through a library, at least in the first instance; in this way you can see if you like it before deciding to own a copy.

ALSO BY KATE WEST

Pagan Paths, Pagan Media Ltd, 1997. Six pathworking cassettes covering the Elements, the Goddess and the God.

Pagan Rites of Passage, Mandrake Press, 1997. A series of booklets giving information and Rituals for the Rites of Passage of Handfasting, Naming and the Rites of Withdrawal.

The Real Witches' Handbook, HarperCollins, 2000. Real Witchcraft for real people with real lives, this book shows how to practise the Craft in a way sensitive to those around you.

The Real Witches' Kitchen, HarperCollins, 2002. Oils, lotions and ointments for Magic and to relieve and heal. Soaps and bathing distillations for Circle and Magical work. Magical incenses, candles and sachets to give or to keep. Food and drink to celebrate the Sabbats, for personal wellbeing and to share with friends.

A Spell in your Pocket, HarperCollins, 2002. A handy pocket-sized giftbook for the Witch on the move.

The Real Witches' Book of Spells and Rituals, HarperCollins, due 2003. A comprehensive grimoire with: Rituals for the Sabbats, Esbats and other phases of the Moon; Rites of Passage, of healing, growth and development; Spells for use in all areas of living in today's world.

GENERAL BOOKS ON THE CRAFT

JW Baker, *The Alex Sanders Lectures*, Magickal Childe, 1984. A perspective on Alexandrian Witchcraft.

Rae Beth, *Hedgewitch*, Phoenix, 1990. Solitary Witchcraft, written as a series of letters to newcomers.

Janice Broch and Veronica MacLer, *Seasonal Dance,* Weiser, 1993. New ideas for the Sabbats.

Janet and Stewart Farrar, *A Witches' Bible* (formerly *The Witches' Way* and *Eight Sabbats for Witches*). Phoenix, 1996. Alexandrian Craft as it is practised.

Gerald Gardner, *The Meaning of Witchcraft*, Rider & Co, 1959; reissued by Magickal Childe, 1991. Gardnerian Witchcraft.

Pattalee Glass-Koentop, *Year of Moons, Season of Trees*, Llewellyn, 1991. Information on the Tree calendar and ideas to incorporate at the Full Moons.

Paddy Slade, *Seasonal Magic*, Capall Bann, 1997. A perspective on Traditional Witchcraft. (Previously published as *Natural Magic.*)

Doreen Valiente, *ABC of Witchcraft*, Hale, 1973. Gardnerian Craft written in 'dictionary' form.

Doreen Valiente, *The Charge of the Goddess*, Hexagon Hoopix, 2000. A collection of poetry and thoughts from the 'Mother of Modern Witchcraft'. Compiled and published after her death, this work gives a unique insight into the development of the modern Craft.

BOOKS ON PARTICULAR
ASPECTS OF THE CRAFT

Anne Llewellyn Barstow, *Witchcraze*, HarperCollins, 1995. Detailed history of the persecution of Witches.

Jean Shinola Bolen, *Goddesses in Everywoman*, HarperCollins, 1985. A guide to finding the Goddess within, and a wealth of tales about the aspects of the Goddess.

Scott Cunningham, *The Complete Book of Oils, Incenses and Brews*, Llewellyn, 1989. Magical preparation and use of oils, incenses and other mixtures.

Scott Cunningham, *Cunningham's Encyclopaedia of Crystal, Gem and Metal Magic*, Llewellyn, 1988. Magical properties of most gemstones available today.

Scott Cunningham, *Cunningham's Encyclopaedia of Magical Herbs*, Llewellyn, 1985. Magical uses, and tales surrounding most common herbs.

Janet and Stewart Farrar, *The Witches' God*, Hale, 1989. Examination of some of the more common Gods.

Janet and Stewart Farrar, *The Witches' Goddess*, Hale, 1987. Examination of some of the more common Goddesses.

Marian Green, *A Calendar of Festivals*, Element Books, 1991. Descriptions of festivals, not just Pagan or Wiccan, around the year with practical things to do, make and cook.

Mrs M Grieve, *A Modern Herbal*, Jonathan Cape, 1931; reissued Tiger, 1992. A detailed reference for the serious herbalist; identification, preparation and use of herbs, ancient and modern. Also available on the internet at *http://www.botanical.com/botanical/mgmh/mgmh.html*.

Paul Katzeff, *Moon Madness*, Citadel, 1981. A study of the effects of the Moon with many of the legends and the mythology associated with it. Not an easy read, but well worth the effort.

Patricia Monaghan, *The Book of Goddesses and Heroines*, Llewellyn, 1981. A definitive guide to major and minor Goddesses from around the world.

Jeffrey B Russell, *A History of Witchcraft*, Thames & Hudson, 1983. A factual history of the Craft.

Egerton Sykes, *Who's Who Non-Classical Mythology*, Oxford University Press, 1993. A dictionary of Gods and Goddesses.

Tybol, *Tybol Astrological Almanac*. Annual Publication. Diary containing detailed astrological information, Goddess and God festivals of different pantheons and from many belief systems, Magical terms and much more.

Bill Whitcomb, *The Magician's Companion,* Llewellyn, 1993. Possibly the 'ultimate' reference work for correspondences and symbols.

OTHER PUBLICATIONS
WHICH MAY BE OF INTEREST

Children of Artemis, *Witchcraft and Wicca,* top quality bi-annual magazine written by Witches for Witches. Articles, poetry, Rituals, spells, art, crafts and events, and much more. Available at *www.witchcraft.org*.

Clarissa Pinkola Estes, *Women who Run With the Wolves,* Rider, 1993. This is not a book on the Craft. However, it discusses the hidden meanings behind many tales and fables, and as such it opens the mind to the interpretation of stories which may have suffered through time and translation. Whilst this 'self-help' book is written for women it does have relevance for both genders.

Terry Pratchett, *Witches Abroad, Wyrd Sisters, Masquerade, Lords and Ladies, etc.* Published by Corgi Books. I recommend these books for their powers of relaxation and the regeneration of a sense of humour after a hard day. They are pure fiction and give a humorous perspective on the world of fictitious (?) Witches (although Granny Weatherwax and Nanny Ogg do have much to guide the aspiring Witch)!

POINTS OF CONTACT

The following organizations facilitate contact, or provide information on Witchcraft and Paganism. Please always enclose a stamped addressed envelope, and remember that some of these organizations may not allow membership to people under the age of 18 years. For further information on getting in touch safely with other Witches or Groups please read the advice in Chapter Four of this book, and that in *The Real Witches' Handbook.*

The Children of Artemis. Initiated Witches who seek to find reputable training
  Covens for genuine seekers. Their magazine *Witchcraft and Wicca* is certainly
  the best on the Craft today. BM Box Artemis, London WC1N 3XX.
  http://www.witchcraft.org (contact@witchcraft.org)
ASLaN. Information on the care and preservation of Sacred Sites all over Britain.
  http://www.symbolstone.org/archaeology/aslan. (andy.norfolk@connectfree.co.uk)
The Hearth of Hecate. The author's group of Covens.
  http://www.pyewacket.demon.co.uk
The Witches' Voice. One of the best American sources of information about the
  Craft. PO Box 4924, Clearwater, Florida 33758-4924, USA.
  http://www.witchvox.com

Inform. Totally independent and not aligned to any religious organization or group. Their primary aim is to help people through providing them with accurate, objective and up-to-date information on new religious movements, alternative religions, unfamiliar belief systems and 'cults'. Houghton Street, London WC2A 2AE. 020 7955 7654.

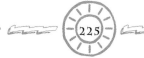

THE REAL WITCHES' HANDBOOK

KATE WEST

A complete introduction to the craft for both young and old alike

A down-to-earth introduction to Witchcraft that gives plenty of practical advice on becoming a wiccan. Whether you want to join a group or work as a Solitary this is an invaluable guide to the wiccan lifestyle.

The chapters will include:

* Myth and Reality – what being a witch is all about, how it compares with the Hollywood image
* What Witchcraft is – the beliefs and practices
* Moon worship, the elements, Gods and Goddesses, the cycles of death and rebirth
* The Sabbats and the Wheel of the Year
* Becoming a Witch – what does it involve?
* Magic – how it works and the responsibilites involved. How to avoid potential danger
* Spellcraft – how to help you pass exams, attract partners, improve family relationships
* Herbal work – herbs for skin, hair, scents, traditional recipes